Art Glass Boxes

A How-to & Reference Manual

By Jack & Trudy Thomas

Aurora Publications
6214 Meridian Avenue
San Jose, California 95120
(408) 997-0437

PATTERNS

 1. THE BASIC BOX

2. SMALL NOTION BOX

 3. KEEPSAKE

4 . SIMPLICITY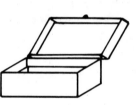

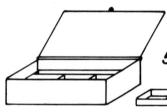 5. DELUXE

6. CUSTOM DELUXE

 7. MEMORIES

8. RECIPE BOX

 9. FANSHELL BOX

10. CLAMSHELL BOX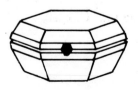

Table of Contents

CREDITS

The 10 patterns in this book are shown as completed projects on the covers. The box in the upper right corner of the front cover and all nine of the boxes on the inside front and back cover have patterns included in this book. Sorry, space did not permit us to include the box top patterns. These boxes were all made by Trudy and Jack Thomas.

The blue bevel top box on the front cover and the similar box in gold crackle glass on the back cover were both made by Scott E. Caldwell.

Gloria Stewart, of Glorious Glass Studio in San Jose, created the open box on the front cover. She also made the tall pink box, the box with the dried flowers in the top, and the open green box which are all on the back cover.

List of Illustrations

(Continued on next page)

Introduction 1

The contents of this book will enable the stained glass artist to create a wide variety of boxes in an easy, "fool proof" method. The successful construction of stained glass boxes offers the craftsman not only great satisfaction but can also prove to be a lucrative enterprise. The market for innovative boxes is great, the uses of stained glass boxes are many, and the styles are virtually limitless.

In the years that I have been doing stained glass, some of the most interesting and challenging projects have been the design and construction of specialty boxes. Many of you are familiar with the standard six piece jewelry box, consisting of a piece of mirror for the bottom, four rectangular pieces for the sides, and a flat lid. Maybe you have varied it by adding a partition or decorative lid. Few people venture beyond that. I intend to show you how to go far beyond that point.

The design of Boxes can be exciting and very creative. Drawers, dividers, trays, and compartments can easily be designed and built. Boxes need not only be rectangular. I will help you design multi-sided boxes, boxes with sloped sides, and boxes with structural lids.

Gift Ideas

The intricacies of a box design is limited only by your imagination. Boxes can be made to suit either men or women. They need not necessarily be designed exclusively for jewelry. How about a box for recipes and coupons, or perhaps a display box for a keepsake or artifact? An excellent baby gift is a small box for diaper pins with a birth announcement laminated into the top.

Men enjoy not only a box for their jewelry, but truly appreciate a box for their desk with compartments for rubber bands, paper clips, pens, pencils, etc. What about a small index style box for business cards? Lids can be decorated with an initial or company logo.

Kids love a box for collectables. A lid may be made to announce the contents of the box. My daughter collects unicorn jewelry and I have made her a large box with a unicorn head on the lid. My son has a large collection of old baseball cards. I made him a large index box with a ball and bat on the lid.

A great gift for teachers is a desk top box with a few compartments to hold all of those things that often clutter their desks. You can even decorate the lid with an apple or a little red school house. A card player will love a box made to hold two decks of cards. I could go on and on. With a little thought, the right box can be made for any occasion.

Great Income Opportunities

Many of you have been looking for a way to make your hobby pay for itself. Stained glass boxes offer a chance for you to do this. Many holiday and gift boutiques are looking for high quality, innovative items. Since boxes make an excellent gift, customers are plentiful. The more varied and creative your designs are, the larger the market. Because boxes are small, the material cost is relatively low. This enables the craftsman to go into a show with a varied and plentiful stock, yet with low investment. Many people buy three or four boxes at holiday time for special personal gifts. Often you will find the same customers come back time after time for special gifts.

The established stained glass craftsman often finds that the sale of boxes give them their "bread and butter" money. Many people cannot afford high priced window panels or lamps, yet they love beautiful hand-crafted items. These people become loyal and appreciative customers.

This book will give you all of the information to improve your box-making skills. I offer information which will enable you to go far beyond the old standby six piece box. Drawers are a unique way to add useful and decorative flair to your box. Trays and compartments allow the craftsman to make a large box with lots of room, yet eliminate the clutter of everything being dumped into one or two large compartments.

Also included in this book are sections that will help you in finishing techniques, hardware selection, tools that simplify box building, and an explanation of recommended materials. New methods of soldering techniques that give your project a highly decorative appearance are explained.

The patterns that are included in this book will give you experience in building many new and innovative designs. Also included is information that will enable you to expand on these designs or create your own.

Tools and Materials 2

Tools

The basic tools used in the construction of glass boxes are the same as in all other stained glass projects: a good glass cutter, soldering iron, and grozing pliers. The other tools used are optional, but surely make the construction of geometric structures easier and more efficient.

The most important optional tool is a glass stripper. I feel that this tool is virtually indispensable. It enables the craftsman to make straight, uniform, and consistent cuts; a must in the construction of boxes.

Running shears are also helpful in the breaking of straight cuts. A *small jewelers or hobbiests saw* (with a close tooth blade) *or craft knife* is used to cut the brass tubing and rod used to make hinges and latches. *Needlenose pliers* help you to make fine, exact bends in the brass rod for your hinges, latches, and drawer pulls.

A *glass grinder* is always a big help in the glass craftsman's workshop. With it you can effectively and quickly clean up all of your glass cuts. Of course, a glass file will suffice as you seldom have much grinding with straight cuts.

A good, flat *work board* with two elevated sides attached to the board at 90 degree angles to each other is very helpful and a must with most glass strippers. Be sure to follow glass stripper manufacturer's specifications as to the height of the sides to be used.

Materials

The materials used are dependent upon the pattern that you select. The patterns contained in this book include a complete materials list. The following sections will give you general information which will help you decide on the best materials for future projects.

50/50 or 60/40 *solder* can be used. 1/4-inch *copper foil* is usually the narrowest foil used, except for possibly some fine line work that might be done in the lid. Wider foil is often used for aesthetic purposes in some projects. I generally use 5/16th-inch foil on the exposed edges at the top edge of the box and the bottom edge of the lid or any edges which might receive a lot of hand contact or which might be subject to stress or pull from hinges, chains or knobs.

One very important material to consider is the *flux* to be used. Many fluxes are too strong and can adversely effect the mirror backing, which is generally used in the bottom of boxes, trays and drawers. Be sure to check with your stained glass supplier for the flux that is safe for use with mirror. For added safety, I dilute the flux with water. I use three (3) parts water to one (1) part of flux. You can experiment with this formula for your specific type of flux. I also apply the flux very sparingly. Never allow it to puddle on the bottom of the box. Never allow the flux to remain on a piece for a long period of time. Frequent washing is recommended. (See the chapter on assembly for special washing procedures.)

The selection of *glass* to be used in the construction of the box is dependent upon the project that you have selected. The following information is generalized and intended to help you in the selection of glass for different areas of your project.

Mirror is frequently used for the bottom of a box, drawer, or tray. Mirror is recommended in these areas as it obscures any structural work which might be done beneath the mirror. A good grade of double strength mirror is recommended because the coating on the back is more resistant to scratches and chemical damage than the backing on most standard mirror tiles. All patterns included in this book utilize double strength mirror. Remember that if double strength mirror is used in the bottom of the box, and the sides of the box are transparent, a wider foil (5/16") must be used on the box side pieces. This obscures view of the edge of the mirror that is used for the bottom.

Single strength, clear window glass is recommended for dividers, support structures and sides of trays and drawers. Antique glass of like thicknesses may also be substituted for clear glass and it can add beautiful color accents to your box. Avoid the ultra-thin antiques, as they can easily break in normal handling. All patterns included in this book call for single strength glass of equal thickness (3/32") to be used for dividers, support structures, and sides of trays and drawers. Substitutions can be made only if consideration and compensations are made for the differences in glass thickness. Double strength glass is ⅛". For an explanation of fraction conversions, see Appendix B.

Some of the illustrations used in this book utilize ⅛" or double strength glass. This has been done for the purpose of illustration only. I recommend the use of single strength glass for dividers, drawer, and tray sides. Single strength glass is easier to cut into narrow strips and makes the finished box considerably lighter.

Opalescent glass is recommended for the sides and top of the box. I prefer to use opalescent glass because it does not allow you to see the many solder lines used in the substructure of the more intricate boxes. Even the more simple boxes with dividers in them look better if you cannot see the lines of the dividers through the sides of the box. I recommend opalescent for the top of most boxes for the same reason. Domes, of course, are best made from single strength clear or antique glass. When selecting an opalescent glass, it is essential that you select a piece of glass that is flat and with a consistent thickness throughout. Glass with a heavy texture can often cause problems in the fitting of pieces. I highly recommend machine rolled, non-textured, opalescent glass for the primary structure of all patterns in this book.

When selecting an opalescent glass, be sure to consider the graining in the glass. Grain running vertically tends to make the box look taller, while grain running horizontally makes the box look shorter, yet larger. Remember, too, that the direction of the glass graining in the sides should be maintained in the lid of the box (see Chapter 8 for further explanation).

Patinas are often used to add a finished effect to the solder work on your box. Patina comes in black or copper color. The black gives a dark grey to black effect. If the solder is polished prior to the application of your patina, a brilliant steel effect can be achieved. The copper patina can turn the solder a wide range of tones from brilliant copper to dark, antique brown. The brighter copper effects are achieved by polishing the solder before and/or after the application of the copper patina. Ask your local stained glass supplier for the proper polish for the project.

The application of these polishes help preserve the sheen of solder bead and guard it against oxidation. Remember, if you are not happy with the patina finish, you may remove the existing finish with a soft, very fine, steel wool and do it again.

There are two different types of *hinges* which are used. The first type is the small hobbiest's brass hinge, which I find to be hard to align and often too bulky and unsightly for effective use on boxes. I prefer to use a piece of brass rod and a piece of brass tubing into which the brass rod snugly fits. In some areas, the brass tubing is available not only in round style, but also square or hexagonal. There are brass rods which are available to fit into all of the above styles. The size of the tubing used is determined by the size and use of the box on which it is to be used.

I do not recommend that a small brass hollow tube be used in lieu of the brass rod, as they often break in shaping or with prolonged use of the hinge. If at all possible, the square or hexagonal tubing is recommended. These tubes allow small gaps to form around the hinge rod, prohibiting any oxidation which may build up within the hinge to lodge and bind up. This oxidation is also minimized if a small amount (about one drop) of light oil lubrication is added to the rod as it is inserted within the tube during the construction of the hinge. Use an oil that will not cause a chemical reaction with the brass.

Many glass suppliers offer a wide selection of brass pieces designed for use as *legs, pulls, knobs, and latches*. If you want a slightly different effect, you can utilize jewels, stones, or shells for the above. You may also form interesting shapes with 16 gauge copper wire and needlenose pliers. These shapes may be filled in with solder to form butterflies, hearts, flowers, or the shape of your choice.

Many hardware stores also have small brass knobs which can be used. Latches and hasps can be found in hardware or hobby stores, or can be made from brass tubing and rod. These techniques will be discussed in a following section.

Basic Box Construction

The basic box consists of five pieces, four sides and a bottom. The four sides join at 90 degree angles. They are either square or rectangular. Multi-sided boxes will be discussed later.

The key to successful box construction is accuracy in both cutting and measuring. An accurate ruler, containing increments of at least 32nds, and a glass stripper are two tools that make accuracy quite easy. The purpose of an accurate ruler is quite obvious. The value of a glass stripper becomes evident when you have used one. A stripper will enable you to make the accurate and consistently measured cuts that are necessary for success. See Appendix A for an explanation of the use and reading of a ruler.

The techniques used in box construction are quite simple. Once you have determined what size box you want and have selected your glass, simply cut it to the right dimensions, foil and solder. "Easier said than done" you say. Well, not really, if you remember a few basic hints.

The first: if all angles are cut at exactly 90 degrees, the box will always be "square".

The second: always cut the bottom panel when you cut your sides, as the bottom will be used as a jig for the construction of the box. Explanation of this method will follow.

The third: always make sure that your cuts are accurate and clean. Grind all spurs or high spots on the cut edge to ensure this.

The easiest way to explain this procedure is to show you, step-by-step, how to assemble a box that will be 7" wide by 5" deep by 2" tall (these dimensions do not include the lid).

1. Select the glass. Make sure that you select a piece that will enable you to maintain consistent graining throughout the project. All sides should be either vertically grained or horizontally grained.
2. Measure the thickness of the glass used for the side panels. This measurement will be used to calculate the side panel and bottom panel cuts.
3. As an example, let's say the glass you select is 1/8" thick. The length of two sides will be cut at 6³/₄". The other two sides will be cut at a length of 4³/₄". The bottom panel will also be cut to these dimensions, since the bottom fits inside the four sides as shown in the front view of the box in Figure III-1. These dimensions take into consideration that the finished product is to be 5" by 7". This method of construction adds one thickness of glass to either end of the side panel widths, as shown in the top view of the corner construction in Figure III-1.

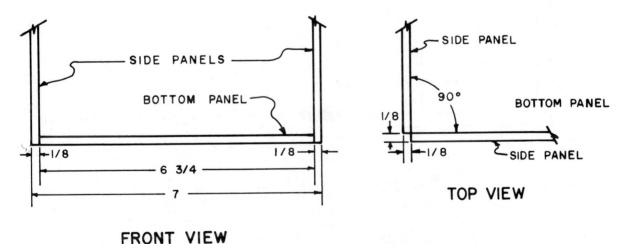

FRONT VIEW

Figure III-1   Front and Top View of Corner Construction

4. After you determine which way you want the grain of the glass to run on the sides of the box, set your glass stripper at 2" and strip off enough strips for the four sides of the box. Be sure that you begin with a straight and smooth edge of glass against the stripper guide rail of the work board. Remember that if your strips are long enough, you might get two sides out of the strip. Figure III-2 shows three pieces of glass which have been cut into 2" strips that are long enough (11") to yield two 4³/₄" pieces and two 6³/₄" pieces for the sides of the box.

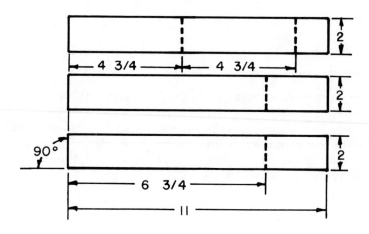

Figure III-2   Measuring Strips of Glass

5. After making sure that the ends of the strip are square (90 degrees) as shown in Figure III-3, set your stripper at 6³/₄". Set the glass strip to be cut at 90 degrees to the bottom edge of the stripper guide. Cut two 6³/₄" lengths. Now, before re-setting the stripper, make a 6³/₄" cut on a piece of glass that you will use as the bottom of the box. The bottom piece of glass or mirror must be cut accurately, as it will become the jig around which the rest of the box is formed.

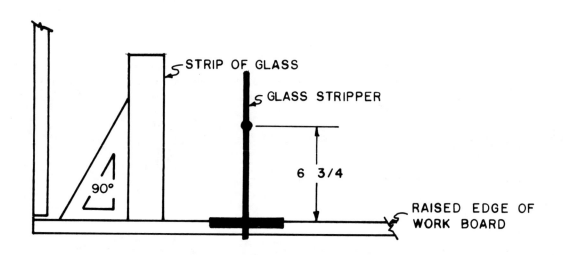

Figure III-3   Cutting Strips to Length

6. Repeat this procedure, setting the stripper at 4³/₄". After this is done, you will have one piece of glass 6³/₄" by 4³/₄", two pieces 2" by 6³/₄", and two pieces 2" by 4³/₄", as shown in Figure III-4.

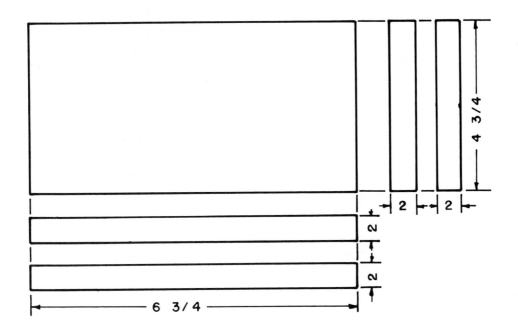

Figure III-4   Five Basic Box Panels

7. Grind all edges to remove any spurs or high spots. Carefully foil all pieces. Be sure that the foil begins and ends on the edge that will be at the bottom of the box.

8. Begin assembly by placing one side panel upright, so that the finished bottom edge of the panel is against the work surface and the raised edge of your work board. Place the bottom (mirror) panel against that side panel and lightly tack at bottom corners. Set another side panel in place against the bottom so that the end meets the first panel. Tack at top and bottom. See Figure III-5 for clarification. Tack remaining two sides in place to form the basic box. The ends of the side panels should meet at the inside edges of the panels. The primary tacks should be at the lower inside corners attaching the side panels to the bottom and to each other. Note the alignment of the glass at the corners. Remember also that the sides are added around the bottom panel, not on top of it.

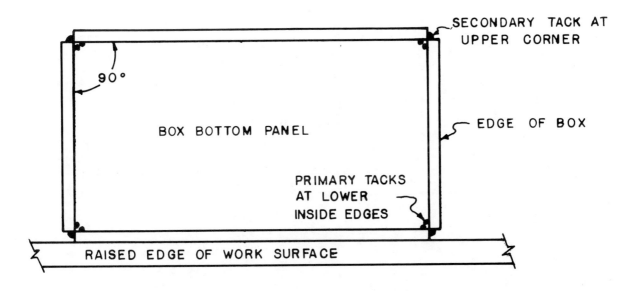

Figure III-5   Primary and Secondary Tack Spots

9. When satisfied with the alignment of the side panels, make secondary tacks at the upper outside corners of the box, as seen in Figure III-5. Look at it again: if everything appears square, final bead the outside of the box. The inside may be beaded only if you are not going to add any compartments. If compartments are to be added, follow the procedures given in Chapter 5. The upper edge of the box may be beaded after the upper edge has been patterned for the lid. See Chapter 8 for this procedure.

10. Washing the box is a very important step. The actual wash procedure is done after it has been wiped clean and patined according to the manufacturer's recommendations. As I have mentioned in the preceding chapters, it is of great importance to effectively clean the box, especially the mirror used in the structure.

It is essential to thoroughly remove all chemical contaminants that might effect the glass and mirror. Since flux is an acid, I advise using a base rinse to neutralize the acid. A simple base rinse can be made by mixing a tablespoon of baking soda with four (4) cups of water (increase the amount of baking soda if greater quantities of water are used). This base mixture is applied by pouring about half of the liquid into the box, tray or drawer. The other half is poured into a shallow container that is large enough to accommodate the bottom of the structure to be cleaned. (I have found that a large glass rectangular cake pan works well for this purpose.) Allow the structure to soak for about three (3) minutes in the pan of solution.

Follow this rinse with a thorough detergent wash. Most dishwashing liquids (those not containing lanolin) are good for this procedure. Thoroughly rinse the structure with warm water. Towel dry, carefully removing all water from the inside corners of the structure. If moisture remains between the inside framework and the sides of the box, you can use a blow dryer, set on medium, to quickly dry the moisture.

Additional cleaning and polishing can be done with a good profesional glass cleaner that is free of ammonia. The patined solder beads may be further polished with a good light metal polish. Ask your stained glass supplier for a product that might be recommended for his procedure.

The basic box is now complete. This procedure is used for all box construction. It ensures a "square" structure every time, if all steps are followed.

Soldering and Finishing Techniques 4

Throughout the preceding sections I have repeatedly mentioned "final beading" at seam or edge. For many of you who have done primarily flat or leaded work, beading structures is often quite frustrating. The most important thing to remember in beading a structure is that in order to achieve a smooth and even bead, it is necessary to keep the seam that you are soldering horizontal, as shown in Figure IV-1.

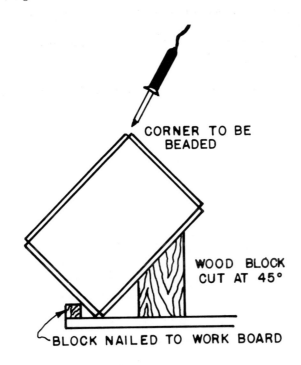

Figure IV-1   Ideal Position for Soldering Corners

I find that by keeping a supply of wooden blocks and wedges around, I am able to prop almost any structure into a good position to solder. Care must be taken not to knock over a structure when working on it. Make sure that it is securely propped up. Do not go off and leave it; always set it back down flat on the work surface. This is especially important if you have small children or pets, or live next to an elevated train or close to the San Andreas Fault.

When beading the outside seams, between side panels, gradually build up your bead. Do not expect to be able to add a large quantity of solder at one time-it will probably drop through the seam. Be patient, do not expect it to be perfect the first time. With a little practice you will be able to achieve the effect that you want. See Figure IV-2.

There are two types of beading techniques used in stained glass. The first, a smooth rounded bead, is most often used on flat work. It can be used on structures, but is often quite hard to achieve due to the fact that you are working with seams that meet at different angles. It is often quite difficult to achieve an even flow when changing directions or planes.

In order to achieve a smooth, well rounded bead on a box, you must be very patient. It is imperative that the line to be soldered be positioned completely horizontally.

The solder is applied in small amounts until all but major gaps have been filled and the entire seam has been build up to slightly less than the desired height. The final rounded bead is achieved by placing an initial amount of solder (about ⅛") at the beginning of your built up seam and allowing it to flow over the immediate area. If the seam is wide, it might be necessary to use a little more solder. The determination of that amount will come with practice. The second drop of solder is added directly next to the first. It is allowed to flow back into the first. This process is continued until the entire seam as been completed. With practice, you should be able to create a well rounded, smooth bead with this technique (see Figure IV-2).

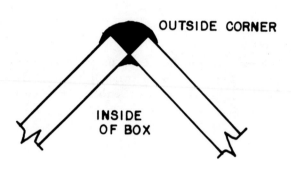

Figure IV-2   Desired Corner Bead

If some bumpiness remains, begin at the end of the seam and quickly and lightly touch the seam at the high spots. Allow the solder to flow a little smoother, creating an even bead, uniform in height. At this time it is advisable to apply a little more flux to ensure a smooth finish. Do not hold the iron in any area for too long, as this can cause the solder to drop through the seam or, worse yet, crack the glass. Should drop-through occur, begin working in another area and allow the first area to cool before continuing.

As with all soldering, practice makes perfect. It takes time to achieve the desired bead. Remember that in order to achieve an even bead, it is important to maintain consistency in the amount of solder that you apply and the rhythm with which you apply it.

The second method I shall refer to as "decorative" soldering. This bead is of a non-smooth, irregular texture. When patined and polished it gives you areas of brilliant highlights. Corners and intersections of angles pose no problem with this bead because irregularity of texture is what is desired.

This method also takes practice to perfect. You want the uneven texture to remain consistent throughout the seam. Many different patterns can be achieved with this decorative bead method. I will explain the two most popular, the "bamboo" effect and the "herringbone" effect. For a more detailed explanation of these and many other techniques, I recommend the book titled "Decorative Soldering for Stained Glass, Jewelry, and Other Crafts", published by Aurora Publications.

As you read the text, refer to the illustrations provided as demonstration is the best teacher. The execution of these methods depend somewhat on the type and temperature of the iron that you use. With a little experimenting, you will be able to adapt the method to your equipment. The iron that I use is a 45 watt, 1000 degree, with a ¼" iron clad chisel tip. I find this style to be adequate for all types of structural construction.

Unlike the smooth bead, allowing the solder to flow evenly into itself is not desired. The decorative bead depends on the new solder cooling before it reaches the preceding portion of the bead line.

The "bamboo" effect is achieved by first light tinning the entire seam to be beaded. Reapply the normal amount of flux to this line. Next, take about ⅛" of solder from your source and apply it to the tinned surface, allowing it to cover an area about ¼" long, as shown in Figure IV-3.

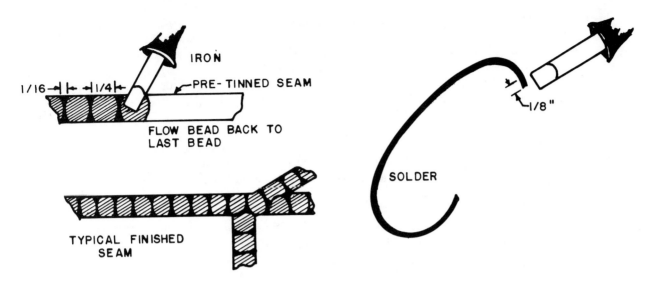

Figure IV-3   Bamboo Bead Technique

You should be holding the tip with the long edge of the chisel running parallel with the line to be soldered. The iron is held at a 45-degree angle to the solder line. The solder should be applied to the center of the tinned line. Again, pick up ¹/₈" of solder from the source and apply it to a point about ¹/₁₆" from the first solder bead. The second bead of solder should flow back, toward the first, cooling as it moves, and end at the end of the first. There should be no gap, but the difference should be distinct. If the second bead flows too smoothly into the first, then you should increase the distance between beads or cut down slightly on the amount of solder used. Continue this process until you have reached the end of the seam.

Turn the structure so that the next seam is horizontal to you and begin the same process, moving away from the intersection. This process is continued until all seams have been completed.

Edges are done in the same manner. Be careful, on edges, to use only enough solder to give a nice, rounded effect. Too much solder will cause unsightly globs on one side of the edge.

When cleaning the patined bead, you should buff it vigorously yet gently, to bring out the highlights. Polishing with a light metal polish can accent these highs even further.

The "herringbone" effect is achieved with a little more work. Again, completely tin the seams to be beaded. The amount of solder used for each application is decreased to about ¹/₁₆". It is picked up and applied with the corner of the chisel tip. The first bead is applied to one side of the line to be beaded. The second is applied to the other side of the bead line very close to the first bead. The solder should flow in a triangular pattern up to the edge of the first, as shown in Figure IV-4.

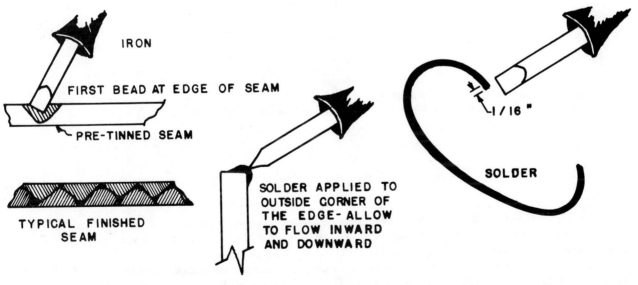

Figure IV-4   Herringbone Bead Technique

This process is continued, moving from side to side, until the entire line is complete. You should have attained a zig-zag effect on your line. Be patient; this technique takes a lot of practice. You need a very quick and light touch. When doing edges in this technique, you must touch only the outer edge of the glass and allow the solder to flow inward and downward. Applying patina, washing and polishing is done in the same manner as with the bamboo style.

The beading of edges is probably the most difficult procedure to master. It is important in the construction of boxes to have a good, heavy and even bead on the edges of boxes, trays, and drawers. If the edges are not well beaded, the foil will often pull away from the glass with use.

Patience and practice are again the key to learning to successfully bead an edge. Another thing to remember is to work with small amounts of solder. Too much solder causes the bead to fall off the edge or creates large, irregular globs on the sides of the edge. Do not be afraid to re-flux the edges, as this helps the solder to spread evenly.

The procedure for beading an edge is simple. Place the edge to be soldered in a horizontal position. Completely tin the front and back edges of the foil. Flux again, and begin at one end of the edge. Apply a small amount of solder (about $1/8''$) to the upper (horizontal) plane of the edge, allowing the solder to flow down onto the front and back planes of the edge. Apply a second drop of solder directly next to it, allowing it to flow into the first. Repeat this process until all of the edge has been beaded. You should have a finished bead that resembles a "U" channel of lead, as shown in Figure IV-5.

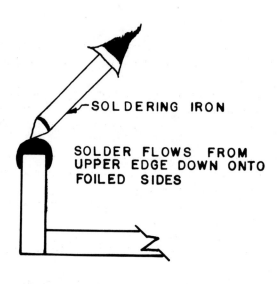

SOLDERING IRON

SOLDER FLOWS FROM UPPER EDGE DOWN ONTO FOILED SIDES

Figure IV-5   Desired Edge Bead

Remove a little solder from any areas which have developed a bulge. If you want to smooth out the entire bead, flux again and begin at one end by touching the solder with the iron until it flows to the desired finish. Be patient and remember "practice makes perfect."

Bottom edges of boxes, trays, and drawers are done in much the same manner as the upper edges, as shown in Figure IV-6. Turn the structure over on the work surface, flux and tin the surface to be beaded. When it has been tinned, flux again and proceed as you did with the upper edge.

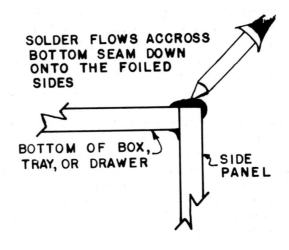

SOLDER FLOWS ACCROSS
BOTTOM SEAM DOWN
ONTO THE FOILED
SIDES

BOTTOM OF BOX,
TRAY, OR DRAWER

SIDE
PANEL

Figure IV-6   Desired Bottom Edge Bead

Make sure that you leave no high spots on the bead, as this may cause the box to sit unevenly. If legs are to be added to the box, be sure to attach them before you final bead the lower edge of the box. Always heavily reinforce, with solder, the points at which you have attached the legs to the box.

After beading has been completed, it is time to patina your structure. I recommend applying patina before washing structure. I wipe off all excess flux and residue from the structure to be patined, as this assures an even coloration of the bead.

A light application of metal polish prior to the patina process will usually give you a lighter, more metallic finish to your patined bead.

If the bead has been finished for a few days before the patina is to be applied or has been washed frequently, it is advisable to polish the solder bead or lightly buff it with a very fine steel wool. This is necessary because oxidation often quickly builds on untreated solder, causing an uneven effect when the bead is patined.

A thorough washing is recommended shortly after the application of the patina. A patined bead may further be polished after washing with metal polish and a brisk buffing with a soft cloth.

Thorough cleaning is one of the most important factors in the overall beauty of the project. I wash the mirrored projects frequently during construction in order to prevent the acid in the flux from contaminating the mirror (see the section on flux in Chapter 2 for further explanation).

The final wash is done when the project has been completed (see Step 10, Basic Box Construction, Chapter 3, for details on a neutralizing rinse for the acid flux). I immerse the entire structure in a warm, sudsy, detergent bath. If you have made a lid with a sandwich type construction, I recommend against immersing the lid, as some moisture can creep between the two panels of glass and ruin the lid.

Completely rub the structure, inside and out, with a sponge until all residue has been removed. Pay special attention to the corners. Thoroughly rinse with warm water.

Drying a box with a lot of small compartments requires the use of paper towels which can get into the small corners and compartments. Be sure to thoroughly dry all surfaces, as water spots are hard to clean off. A brisk towel drying will add a beautiful luster to the bead. For hard-to-reach spots between the support dividers and the sides of the box, you may want to use a blow dryer, set on medium heat, to remove all moisture.

A good professional glass cleaner is recommended for final touch-ups. These are usually available at your stained glass supplier's shop. I strongly recommend against the use of glass cleaner with a high ammonia content, as this can cause unsightly oxidation of the solder bead.

A lovely finishing touch for the box is the addition of felt or leather to the bottom of the box, tray, or drawer. If you anticipate doing this, be sure to compensate for the thickness of these additions when constructing those things to which they will be attached. These pads can be attached with rubber cement, white glue, or rubber silicone sealant.

Compartments 5

I use compartments in two ways. The first and most common is to divide the large area within the box into smaller, more organized areas with full compartment dividers. This is done by cutting strips of glass the height of the inside wall of the box by the length or width of the box, foiling them, and tacking them at the desired positions within the box. The formula for determining the sizes of these strips will be discussed later.

The second type is support dividers, which are used to support trays as well as to divide the area. These dividers are shorter than the height of the sides of the box and run around the entire inside perimeter of the box as well as across it. The use of trays in boxes offers the opportunity to divide deep boxes into small, organized areas. The construction of trays will be discussed in the next section.

The illustration shown in Figure V-1, should help you make the necessary measurements for typical full compartment dividers in a box that measures 5" deep by 7" wide by 2" high. The glass used in the sides and bottom of the box is 1/8" thick. The divider glass is also 1/8" thick. These measurements are all helpful in determining the sizes of the dividers. I have used 1/8" glass in the dividers for illustration purposes only. The patterns included in this book use 3/32" (single strength) glass. You may substitute 1/8" double strength in the patterns, but you must alter the patterns to compensate for the added thickness.

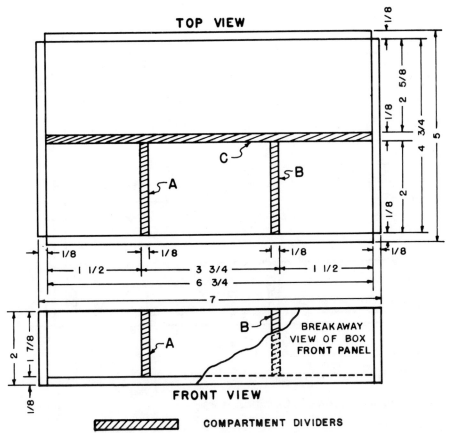

Figure V-1   Full Compartment Dividers

Panels "A", "B", and "C" are divider panels. Panel "C" runs the full width and height of the inside of the box. It is cut at the same length as the side panel of the box itself. Its height is the height of the side panel minus the thickness of the bottom panel. Panels "A" and "B" can be cut at any length to place the "C" panel at any desired position. If the "A" and "B" panels are cut at 2", they position the "C" panel in the approximate center of the box. The height is again determined by the height of the side panels minus the thickness of the bottom panel.

Support dividers used in conjunction with compartment dividers are shown in Figure V-2. The illustration should help you make the necessary measurements for dividers that could support one or more trays in a box that is 8" deep by 10" wide by 4" high. The glass used in the side dividers and bottom is 1/8" thick. These measurements are helpful in determining the sizes of the dividers. The support dividers are labeled "A", "B", "C", and "D". The full compartment dividers are "E" and "F".

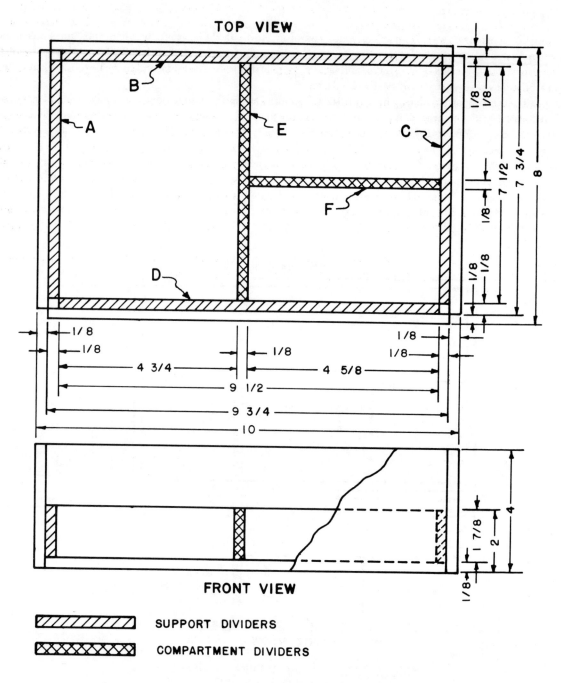

Figure V-2   Support Dividers

In support dividers, which are set around the inside perimeter of the box, the formula for figuring the length of each divider strip is the length of the box side panel, itself, minus two thicknesses of the glass used for the support dividers, minus $1/32$" to compensate for foil and any slight cutting error that might occur. For example, in Figure V-2, support dividers "B" and "D" would be cut at $9^{15}/32$". That is $9^3/4$" minus $2/8$" minus $1/32$".

Support divider panels "A" and "C" are then calculated at $7^3/4$" minus $2/8$" minus $1/32$". This means that these two panels are cut at a length of $7^{15}/32$". The compartment "E" divider is cut the same length as the "A" and "C" support dividers. The compartment "F" divider is cut at an arbitrary length to enable you to position the "E" panel where you want it. If you desire to locate the "E" panel in the center of the box, you would cut the "F" panel a length of $4^5/8$" (half the $9^1/2$" internal width minus $1/8$" for the thickness of the glass of "E" panel).

The height of both compartment and support divider panels is determined by the height of the box sides and the height of the tray that you may want to put on top of them. If the sides of the box are 4" and the bottom mirror panel of the box is $1/8$" thick and the tray that you want to add will be about $1^7/8$" high, the height of the support divider panels should be $1^7/8$". This allows for foil and solder beads on the dividers and tray.

It is not necessary to make drawings this detailed. If you study the plans of the two different types of dividers, both full and support, you will notice that the measurements are all arrived at in the same manner. The only thing that you have to consider is the space into which the dividers must fit.

Lengths of dividers which simply run from side to side or front to back are simply the same length as the support divider sides that they parallel. (Remember to cut about $1/32$" small to compensate for foil and slight cutting error on all panels.) The shorter dividers which further divide the large compartments are cut at arbitrary lengths to achieve the desired effects. They must be attached at both ends at a common measurement from a reference point. That is, if you set a small divider two (2) inches from the left side at the front, be sure that it is also set in two (2) inches at the rear. Do not rely on it looking straight. Use a ruler. Be sure to tin and patina the ends and bottom edge of dividers before attaching them within the box, as you will not get a chance to solder coat them after they are attached and against another piece of glass.

All of this probably sounds very complicated, but after you have begun working with dividers, it will seem logical and simple. Remember that the key is to always take into consideration glass thickness, and allow a little extra ($1/32$") for good measure.

Remember that in preparing a basic box for the installation of dividers, you must do no soldering on the inside seams until after the installation of the dividers. Early soldering interferes with the fit of the dividers.

Trays 6

The advantage of adding trays to boxes is that it enables you to use all space within a box in a very neat and organized manner. If a box is 3" or 4" deep, then the best you could do, without a tray, is to have a lot of small, very deep compartments in which things could get lost or tangled. If that same box had a tray, it would create a lot of small shallow compartments, creating much more usable space.

Boxes with trays give you a finished product that is the ultimate in usefulness. The first thing to remember in creating a tray is that it is simply a box that fits within a box. You must compensate for thicknesses of glass and solder beads in the main box and the tray. Do not cut it to fit snugly within the box, as the final soldering may cause it to bind.

Figure VI-1 is a drawing showing all of the dimensions that you must take into consideration in making a tray. It may look quite complicated, but once again, takes into consideration only a few basic concepts.

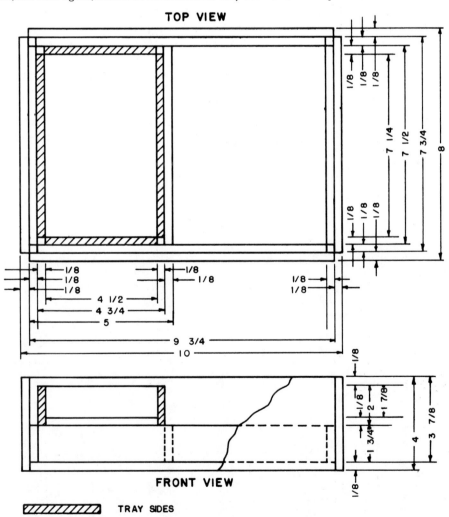

Figure VI-1   Tray Calculations

The tray is a little less than half the width of the box. It is designed to fit on top of the dividers described in the previous chapter. Although the scale of the drawing in the previous chapter are not identical to this drawing, all dimensions are the same.

The key to figuring the dimensions of the tray is knowing the inside dimensions of the dividers already put into the box. Note that on the drawing, the inside dimensions of the compartment (over which the tray will fit) are $4^3/_4$" by $7^1/_2$". Those also are the dimensions of the outside of the tray. This allows for a $^1/_4$" space between each side of the tray and the inside walls of the box. This gap allows for easy removal of the tray. The solder bead on the outside of the tray is sufficient to keep the tray from falling into the bottom compartments of the box. A full solder bead on the tray and on the upper edge of the dividers is recommended.

To determine the height of the side panels of the tray keep in mind that you do not want the tray to reach all the way to the top edge of the box itself. I usually allow about $^1/_4$" clearance at the top of the tray and the top of the box side.

The length of the side panels is determined in the following manner. If the inside dimensions of the dividers upon which you are setting the tray are $4^3/_4$" by $7^3/_4$", then the outside dimensions of the tray should be $4^3/_4$" by $7^3/_4$". To find the panel lengths, simply subtract the thickness of two pieces of glass that are being used for the panel sides from the finished side dimension. Example: if the glass that is being used for the side panels is $^1/_8$", then you must subtract $^2/_8$" ($^1/_4$") from $4^3/_4$". This gives the finished dimension of $4^2/_4$" ($4^1/_2$"). The other dimension is calculated in the same manner. Remember that at the time you cut one length of sides, you should make the first cut for the tray bottom panel. Refer to the basic box construction section for construction methods.

The same principles apply to the construction of a tray that will fit the entire inside perimeter of the box. Two small trays may also be calculated in the same manner. Remember to always take into consideration the fact that you must have some room between the tray and the box to allow easy removal of the tray or trays.

Between the inside framework and the sides of the box, you can use a blow dryer set on medium, to quickly dry the moisture. Additional cleaning and polishing can be done with a good professional glass cleaner that is free of ammonia. The patined solder beads may be further polished with a good light metal polish. Ask your stained glass supplier for a product that might be recommended for this procedure.

The basic box is now complete. This procedure is used for all box construction. It ensures a "square" structure every time, if all steps are followed.

Drawers 7

The addition of a drawer to a box represents the ultimate in box engineering. I recommend attempting a drawer only after you have successfully worked with trays. A drawer is essentially a tray that fits in a separate compartment at the bottom of a box. Preparation for adding a drawer begins with the cutting of the side panels of the box itself, and requires the addition of a second bottom in the box. I will give a step-by-step explanation of the procedures of cutting and assembling a box made to contain a drawer. Boxes with drawers are generally quite large, usually no smaller than 8" wide by 6" deep by 4" high.

1. Select the glass that you want to use for the sides of the box. Remember that opalescent glass is best for this type of project as it will hide all of the sub-structure of the box.
2. Determine what size box you want. Be sure that it will be large enough to accommodate all of the internal structure. The box I will use as an example will be 10" wide by 7" deep by 4" high. All of the glass that I will use will be $1/8$" thick.
3. Be sure to have all of the glass that you will need for the total structure. Glass for the sides, dividers, mirror for the bottom of the tray and the "upper" bottom of the box and the bottom of the drawer. Clear glass may be used for the second bottom that is under the drawer.
4. The techniques for calculating all panel sizes have been given in preceding chapters and therefore will not be elaborated upon in these instructions. I will however, tell you how to make calculations pertinent to the addition of a drawer.
5. Since I have determined that the side panels of the box are to be 4" high I begin by cutting enough 4" strips to construct the box. These strips will be cut into two pieces $9^{3}/_{4}$" long and two pieces $6^{3}/_{4}$" long. Remember that at this time I also cut the two bottoms of the box (1 mirror and 1 clear glass).

The next step is the first in preparing to construct the box to accommodate a drawer. I select which $9^{3}/_{4}$" panel will be used for the front panel of the box. A 1" cut is made along the bottom edge of this panel, giving us one panel 3" by $9^{3}/_{4}$" and one panel 1" by $9^{3}/_{4}$" as shown in Figure VII-1.

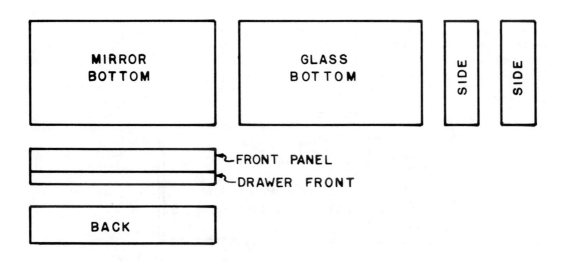

Figure VII-1   Seven Basic Panels in Drawered Box

The 1" panel will be used as the front of the drawer itself. A reference point must now be made on each of the two strips that you have just cut. You should place a mark on each panel in such a manner that you can match them in a future step. The finished structure will look much better if the grains in these two pieces match.

6. Set the 1" panel aside. It is to be used as a drawer front in step 14. After you have made sure that the edges are straight and smooth on the remaining six pieces (4 sides and 2 bottoms), you may foil them.

7. Assembly begins by holding the corners of one side panel and the back panel together and tacking them top and bottom. The two panels should be at 90 degrees to one another. Tack the second side to the other end of the back panel in the same manner.

The front panel must now be added. The edges of the box which are resting on the work surface represent the top edge of the box. The panel which will be the front of the box is added so that the reference point is up away from the work surface and it will match with the drawer front panel when it is in place. When positioned, tack it in place.

8. When all four sides are tacked together, turn the structure over on your work surface. The front of the box should be up off the work surface by 1" and all four upper edges should be even, as shown in Figure VII-2. Make any adjustments necessary.

Foil the two bottom pieces once you have made sure that they are smooth and straight. Place the clear bottom panel to the inside of the box, flat on the work surface. It should fit snugly. Make any adjustments necessary. Lightly tack in place, then add a light bead to the inside bottom seam, around the clear bottom.

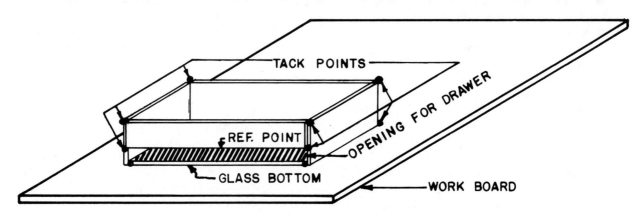

Figure VII-2   Assembly of Box, Front View

9. The second, mirror bottom, must now be added. This requires finding something that will hold the mirror bottom in place, as shown in Figure VII-3. You will need something $7/8$" thick to serve as a spacer. A couple of blocks of wood cut to this size work well. You may also use books or magazines, scraps of glass, or anything that will hold the bottom evenly in place. It is wise to check the measurements down from the upper corner edges of the box before tacking. When all is aligned, lightly tack in place. Do not add a bulky bead to the inside of the box if you are going to add tray support dividers to the inside. If not, you may finish the bead.

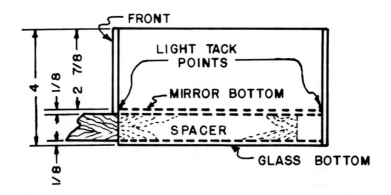

Figure VII-3   Installation of Second Bottom, End View

10. Now add all box interior dividers according to the instructions in the section on dividers and trays.
11. Finish bead the entire box inside and out except for the edges that surround the opening for the drawer.
12. Because the drawer is simply a box within a box, the first thing to do before the actual construction of the drawer begins is to accurately measure the box in which it will fit. You must know the height, width, and depth of the opening of the box into which the drawer will fit. If you refer to the drawing, shown in Figure VII-4, you will note that the opening in the box is $7/8$" high by $9^3/4$" wide by $6^3/4$" deep. Knowing this, I can now begin calculation of the drawer size.

The first and easiest dimension to calculate is the height of the drawer sides. The opening height is $7/8$" so I know that the panel height must be smaller. I must allow for the thickness of the solder bead at the top and bottom of the drawer and the seam at the bottom inside of the box. I generally allow $1/8$" in this situation. That means that the side panels will be cut at a height of $3/4$".

The depth of the drawer is an arbitrary dimension as long as it allows the drawer to fit within the opening. I have chosen to cut the drawer side panels $5^7/8$". This will result in a drawer that will extend into the opening 6", well within the dimensions of the opening.

The most difficult dimension to determine is the width of the drawer. With the knowledge that the opening in the front of the box is $9^3/4$", I begin by making an allowance for the solder bead on either side panel of the drawer and the beads on the bottom inside seams of the opening. I have found that leaving a space of $3/16$" on either side of the drawer allows for the easy movement of the drawer in and out. The formula that is used for determining the back panel of the drawer (remember that the front panel has been cut in a previous step) is therefore: $9^3/4$" minus $6/16$" minus $2/8$", the thickness of the two side panels of the drawer, totaling $9^1/8$". I now have determined all of the drawer panel dimensions and am ready to cut the glass (the bottom, two sides, and back panel).

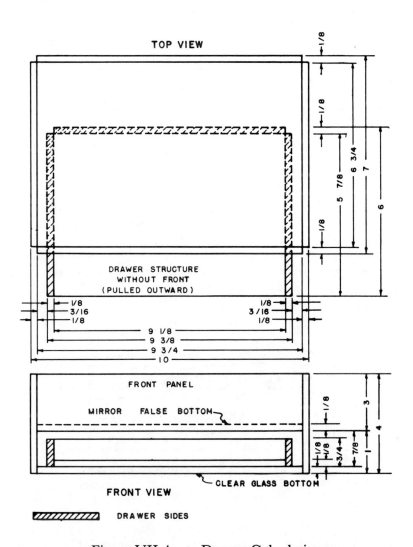

Figure VII-4   Drawer Calculations

13. I am now ready to cut the four remaining pieces of the drawer (the front was cut in Step 5). First, cut your clear glass, for the three sides, into $3/4$" strips. Then cut two of then at a length of $5^7/8$". Remember to make a $5^7/8$" cut on your mirror, for the drawer bottom, at this time. Cut one $3/4$" clear strip at $9^1/8$". Make a $9^1/8$" cut on the mirror. This gives you all of the pieces that you will need for the basic drawer. After you have removed all spurs from the glass, foil all four pieces.

14. The drawer front panel is now ready to foil. This is done in a rather unusual manner, as you must have a large area of foil on the back of the drawer's front on which to attach the drawer itself. The extra foil is attached before the foil is wrapped around the perimeter of the panel. I begin by laying the drawer front, face down, on the work surface and applying strips of foil along the four edges of the back of the panel as shown in Figure VII-5. Press this foil down and then wrap the panel in the usual manner. $1/4$" foil is usually sufficient for the above process.

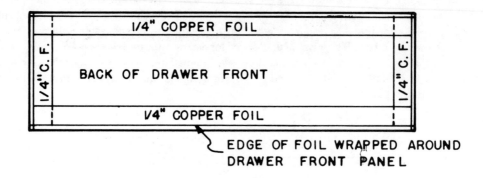

Figure VII-5   Preparation of Drawer Front Panel

15. The drawer is now ready to assemble. Set the front panel aside. Follow box and tray construction procedures to build the box. Remember that the front edges of the bottom and sides must line up. When it is tacked together, slide it in and out of the drawer opening in the box. It will be a little sloppy. If it moves freely, you may final bead the outside seams. Do not bead the inside if you want to add dividers in the drawer.

16. The placing of the front panel on the drawer, so that it will fit the opening at the front of the box, is quite tricky. There is no set formula for this procedure; you might say it is hit and miss. You know that it must be centered with respect to the width. See Figure VII-6. The up and down positioning is what can give you trouble.

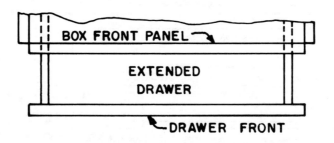

Figure VII-6   Front Top View of Centered Drawer

When fitting the drawer front to the bottom edge of the box front, you must take solder bead thickness into consideration. I generally begin by centering the front edge of the drawer structure on the back of the drawer front panel; lightly tack. Try slipping the drawer in. How does the drawer fit? For ideal positioning, see Figure VII-7. It should be centered with respect to width.

If the gap between the top edge of the drawer and the bottom edge of the front panel of the box is too great, taking into consideration solder bead thickness, then you will have to raise the drawer front slightly. If it appears that the gap will not be enough to accommodate the solder beads, then you should lower the box front slightly.

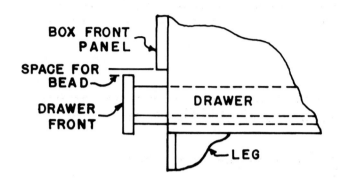

Figure VII-7   Side View of Drawer

If your are having difficulty judging the bead thickness, add a finished bead to the top of the drawer and the bottom edge of the front panel of the box. When all is aligned you will notice that the lower edge of the drawer front will be slightly below the bottom plane of the box. This is normal. Legs are added to the box to compensate for this.

When you are satisfied with the alignment of the front panel with the drawer itself, you may final solder all exposed foil at the back of the drawer front panel. Be careful to add enough solder to secure it well, yet not enough to interfere with the alignment of the drawer when closed. Add solder to all remaining seams and edges at the front opening of the box.

Dividers can now be added to the drawer (see section of dividers). Final bead any remaining edges or seams on the drawer. Add a drawer pull (see Chapter 11), patina and thoroughly wash the drawer.

17. Add legs to the bottom of the box. They need be no higher than 1/2''. If you have not done so already, make any trays for the box. Design, construct, and install a lid. Add a lid lift nob. Wash the entire box according to the washing instructions in the section on finishing techniques.

You are now done and have created a structure of great complexity. CONGRATULATIONS!

Box Tops 8

The box lid offers the craftsman the greatest opportunity for artistic expression. The craftsman can create small window panels to be set into the lid. Many things can be sandwiched between two pieces of glass that will create a very special and highly individualized lid. Polished stones, shells, coins, etc., can be set into a lid for a very unusual effect. The possibilities are almost limitless. The instructions included in this book do not call for specific lid designs; I may, however, recommend one of the three basic styles.

The different lid designs illustrated on the covers of this book are provided to give you ideas to incorporate in your own lid pattern designs. The three basic styles shown in Figure VIII-1 will be discussed later in this chapter. I must now address the problem of how to determine the dimensions of the lid. I generally recommend that the box be constructed first and the lid made to fit it. Constructing a box to fit a lid will be covered a little later. I have found that it proves to be a lot easier to make the lid to fit the box, especially if the sides of the box are not perfectly square.

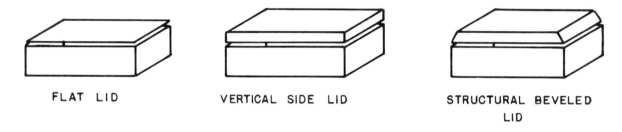

FLAT LID VERTICAL SIDE LID STRUCTURAL BEVELED LID

Figure VIII-1 Three Basic Lid Styles

Since you want the lid to fit on top of the upper edge of the box, one of the easiest ways to assure a perfect fit is to make a template of the upper perimeter of the box itself. This is done by placing the box, upside down, on a piece of pattern paper (be sure that the heavy edge of the box to be templated does not have a heavy solder bead on it) and scribing a line around the edge, as shown in Figure VIII-2. Make sure that the pen scribes close to the edge, otherwise the top could become too large.

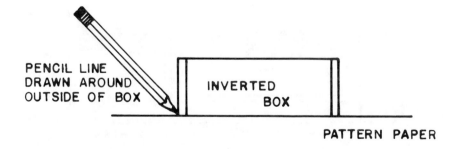

PENCIL LINE DRAWN AROUND OUTSIDE OF BOX

INVERTED BOX

PATTERN PAPER

Figure VIII-2 Patterning Upper Edge of Box

Your lid should be constructed to the inside of the pattern that you have just made. Remember that the scribed side of the pattern will represent the bottom, inside surface of the lid. It is best to mark the pattern "top", "bottom", "front", and "back". Once you have the pattern, you can consider which of the three basic lid construction styles you want to use.

The first and easiest style is the standard flat lid. In addition to making a small window panel to fit within the pattern, the sandwich or inlay methods can create beautiful lids. The important thing to remember with this style is that it must fit within the pattern that you have made. The lid may be completely soldered, top and bottom, except for the back edge. This is where the hinge tube will be attached later. You then proceed with the hinging instructions provided in Chapter 9.

The second lid style I refer to as the vertical-sided lid. The sides are made of equal height strips of glass, usually the same type of glass used on the sides of the box. The width of the strips usually vary from 1/2" to 1". This is not always the case, and it is up to the craftsman. This style can also be varied by making the back strip wider than the front, therefore enabling you to create a slope top lid as shown in Figure VIII-3. The sides of this style lid must be cut to fit from one height to the other. The size (length) of these strips should be the same as the length of the strips of glass used in the box.

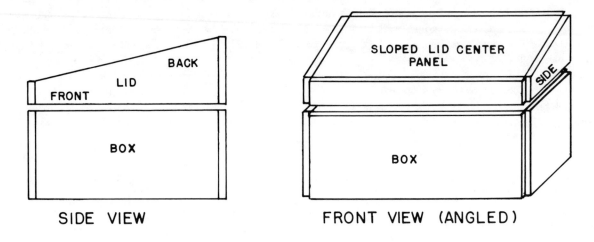

Figure VIII-3   Slope Top Lid

When the four vertical sides of the lid have been cut and foiled, lightly tack them together and make sure that they fit within the pattern of the box lid. Make any adjustments necessary. When you are satisfied with the fit, you should make a pattern for the panel that goes within the four sides. This is done by placing the tacked together sides on the lid pattern, squaring it, and scribing a line along the inside perimeter of the four sides, as shown in Figure VIII-4.

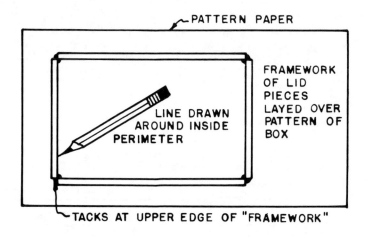

Figure VIII-4   Patterning Center Panel of Vertical Lid

You now proceed by creating a flat panel in the design of your choice (for suggestions, see lid style described in this chapter) to fit within the four vertical sides. Solder all seams and edges except for the bottom back edge and proceed with hinging (Chapter 9).

I refer to the third lid style as "structurally beveled". I have chosen this name because the sides of this lid are angled upward and inward, giving the effect of a bevel. I have provided a pattern for this angle, shown in Figure VIII-5. The strip of glass that I cut this angle from is usually ³/₄" wide. You may, however, want to vary this for specific needs. I do not recommend going much smaller.

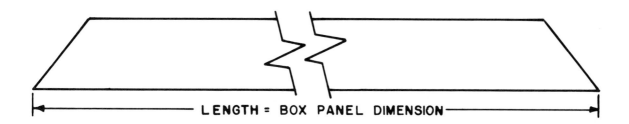

LENGTH = BOX PANEL DIMENSION

Figure VIII-5   Typical Panel for Structurally Beveled Lid

The length of these strips are usually the same as those used in the construction of the box itself. After you have cut and foiled the four angled strips, lightly tack them together, angling the upper edges inward until the angles fit and the bottom edges fit flat on the work surface. Set this "framework" on top of the pattern and check its alignment. Make any squaring adjustments necessary. When you are satisfied with the fit, put a heavy solder bead on the seams sufficient to hold the framework's shape.

Turn the framework upside down on a piece of pattern paper and trace the inside perimeter of the small opening as shown in Figure VIII-6. Make sure that you do not alter the shape of the framework while turning it over or tracing the pattern. You now proceed by creating a flat panel in the style of your choice to fit within the four angled sides. See the section on flat lid design for suggestions.

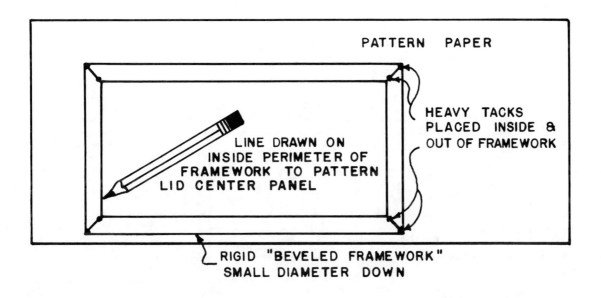

PATTERN   PAPER

HEAVY TACKS
PLACED INSIDE &
OUT OF FRAMEWORK

LINE DRAWN ON
INSIDE PERIMETER OF
FRAMEWORK TO PATTERN
LID CENTER PANEL

RIGID "BEVELED FRAMEWORK"
SMALL DIAMETER DOWN

Figure VIII-6   Patterning Center Panel of Structurally Beveled Lid

When you have completed the flat panel, install it within the four sides of the lid. It is best to only tack it in place until you have checked the alignment of the lid on the box. Make any adjustments necessary. When you are satisfied with the fit, you may final bead the entire lid with the exception of the lower back edge of the lid. This is where you will attach the hinge tube. Proceed with hinging process detailed in the section on hinging (Chapter 9).

The main thing to remember in making successful box lids is care. Always measure accurately and pattern exactly. Remember to always check that the lid fits flat on the box before you final solder bead. When beading, be sure to put a heavy bead on the lower edge of the lid because the foil has a tendency to pull away from the glass with prolonged handling.

Designing Boxes to Fit the Lid

In the event that you have something specific that you want to use for a box lid, you can, with a few calculations, determine the sizes for the sides of the box. Three different formulas are used, depending on which of the three lid styles you choose.

Flat Lids

If you choose a flat panel as the lid, the length of one side will equal the dimension of the corresponding side of the lid minus two (2) thicknesses of the glass you choose for the box. This is illustrated in Figure VIII-7.

For example, if the flat panel measures 5" by 7" and the glass you have chosen for the sides measure 1/8"thick, then the 5"side will actually measure 5" minus $^2/_8$", or $4^3/_4$". The 7" side will actually measure 7" minus $^2/_8$", or $6^3/_4$". That means that you would cut two sides $6^3/_4$" and two sides $4^3/_4$" long. The height of the box is up to you.

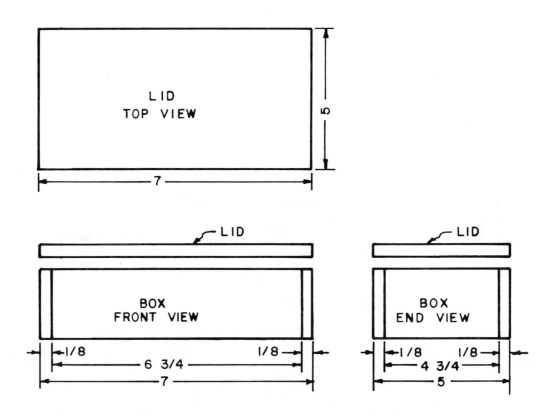

Figure VIII-7   Patterning for Flat Style Lid

Vertical Side Lid

The second formula is used when a vertical sided lid is constructed first. The sides of a vertical sided lid are cut to the same dimensions as the lid center panel. This measurement is also used for the sides of the box. For example, if the panel is 5" by 7", the lid side strips and the sides of the box will be cut at 5" and 7" lengths. If the glass that you are using for the box and its sides is 1/8" thick, then the total finished size of the box will be 5 1/4" by 7 1/4", as shown in Figure VIII-8.

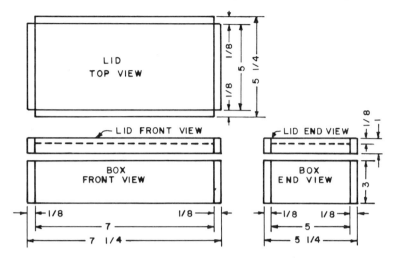

Figure VIII-8   Patterning for Vertical Side Style Lid

Structurally Beveled Top

The third method is not really a formula, but a procedure. This method is used to determine the sides of a box with a structurally beveled top. This would occur if you wanted to surround a 3" by 5" panel with a structurally beveled frame. Once you have accurately measured the panel, refer to the angle pattern shown in Figure VIII-9. You must first determine how wide a strip you want to use for the sides of the lip. If you choose a 3/4" strip, cut one end at the patterned angle. Then measure 3" from the upper corner of the angle down the top edge of the strip and mark a point. Using the other end of the angle template, cut the angle down and away from that point. This will give you one side. Repeat the process using the same measurement for the second 3" side. The same process is again used measuring 5" across the top edge to make the remaining two sides. The sides of the box should be the same measurement as the longest dimension at the bottom of each corresponding angled strip, as shown in Figure VIII-9.

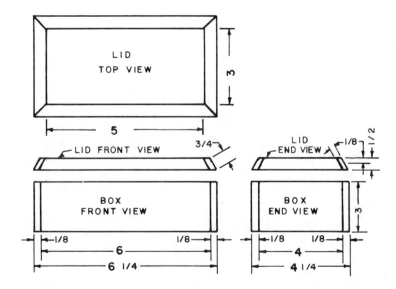

Figure VIII-9   Patterning for Structurally Beveled-Style Lid

If any measurement other than $3/4''$ is used in the side strip of a structurally beveled lid, the overall dimension of the box will change. I suggest making a drawing of the altered side strip. The measurement of the longest part of this strip will become the measurement of the corresponding box side.

Hinges, Latches, and Hasps

Hinging is often the most difficult part of the assembly of a box. There are many different problems which may arise. Breakage and mis-alignment are the two most common problems. The methods I use vary, and greatly depend on the type and size of the project. The material used depends on the weight of the door or lid. In the following section, I will describe various hinging and latching methods that I have found effective. I will describe the materials and sizes I use for specific situations. You may have to vary these in future projects, depending upon their size and availability of certain materials.

I will first address the problem of hinges. The hinges are basically made up of three pieces. A long piece of brass tubing is used to span the entire width of the piece to be hinged (see Chapter 2 for description of types of tubing). I have decided to use one long tube in lieu of two short pieces because this eliminates many alignment problems and gives a more even line to the finished piece. Using one tube also minimizes the chance of flux entering the tube which, with time, causes oxidation within the hinge that can cause it to bind and possibly break. I also like to add a drop of light lubricating oil in to the tube during assembly, as this will further help fight oxidation. In the chapter on materials I have described alternate types of tubing. Round tube is adequate, but the square and hexagonal tubing offers safeguards against oxidation buildup within the tube. The three types of tube are shown in Figure IX-1.

Figure IX-1   Three Tube Types, Rod in Place

The tubing is cut with a small, fine toothed, hobbiest saw or an X-Acto knife. The length is determined by the piece of glass that it is going to be attached to. The exact size varies sometimes with the size of the material used. The larger the diameter of the brass rod, the shorter you cut the brass tube into which it will fit. This is something that can be adjusted as you begin to assemble the hinge. A good starting point is to cut the tube $1/8$ of an inch smaller than the piece of glass to which it is going to be attached. Remember, it is the measurement of the piece of glass, not the total width of the box. The relationship between the tube, the glass, and the box is shown in Figure IX-2.

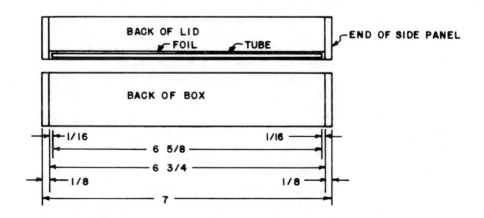

Figure IX-2   Box and Hinge Dimensions

39

Next, cut two pieces of brass rod approximately 1½" long (see Chapter 2 for description of rod to be used). Bend the two pieces into a 90 degree angle as shown in Figure IX-3. The bend should not be in the middle of the hinge rod. I generally begin the bend at the one-half inch point, which leaves the other leg of the angle approximately one inch. The half inch leg will be the part which is inserted into the tube.

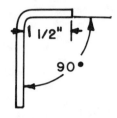

Figure IX-3   Bent Hinge Rod

Before any soldering is done, I must now check the width of the hinge unit. Insert the two short bent rods into both ends of the cut tube. Hold this unit against the edge of the lid of the box as shown in Figure IX-4 for the different types of lids, and lower it into position on the box.

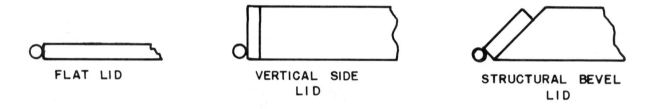

FLAT LID   VERTICAL SIDE   STRUCTURAL BEVEL
                        LID   LID

Figure IX-4   Hinge Tube Placement

The legs should hang down into the back vertical seams of the box as shown in Figure IX-5. If they do not fit into the seam, but extend beyond it, you will have to cut the tubing shorter until they do align with the box seams. Once the proper alignment is achieved, you may tack the tube to the edge of the lid.

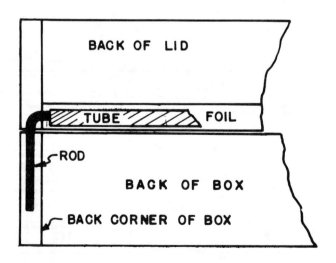

Figure IX-5   Hinge Rod Placement

I recommend tacking about one-half inch in from the ends of the tube. You must always use extreme care not to get any flux or solder near the opening of the tube. Now again insert the short legs of the two angles into the openings at both ends of the tube. Do they still fit down into the seams? If they do not, make any necessary adjustments. If everything lines up, as shown in Figure IX-6, you may now begin the final alignment. Before soldering the legs into the seams of the box, be sure to add one drop of light lubricating oil into the tube.

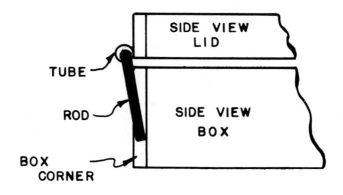

Figure IX-6   Single Bend Rod

You may have to bend the legs slightly to have them fit into the seams exactly. Remember that the most crucial part at this point is that the lid fit flat and squarely on the box. The legs might even have to be bent slightly inward, back towards the box, to achieve a good fit, as shown in Figure IX-7. Sometimes the legs are bent in a zig-zag configuration to achieve the fit. This bending and re-bending is one reason that I like to use solid rod rather than tubing, as it will take more shaping before it breaks.

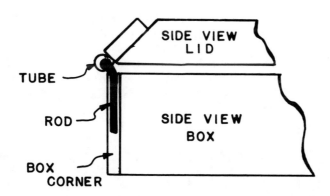

Figure IX-7   Double Bend Rod

When you are completely satisfied with the fit of the lid to the box and with the way that the hinge legs fit into the back seams, you are now ready to final tack the legs in place. Now open and close the lid a couple of times. If it does not bind, you may final bead all seams and edges.

Remember: take special care to keep flux and solder away from the ends of the hinge. Be sure to put an adequate amount of solder bead over the hinge tube and the edge of glass to which it is attached, as the strength of the hinge is dependent on the strength of this bead.

Doors

The addition of doors to boxes occurs in only a few very advanced projects. I have not included a pattern for a box with door in this text, but I feel that the information may be helpful in your future projects. Watch for upcoming Aurora Publication Patterns for some large projects which utilize doors.

When hinging doors, as you may do in future projects, the same procedures are followed. The hinge tube is attached to the door panels and the hinge legs are bent and soldered into the horizontal seams running away from the door opening, as shown in Figure IX-8. Make sure that the bend in the bottom legs are directly against the tube on the door; this will prevent the door from sagging.

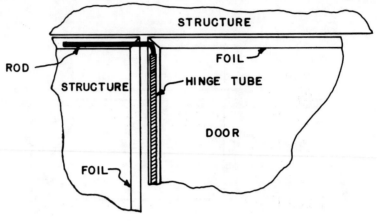

Figure IX-8   Hinged Door

Latches and Hasps

Latches and hasps are used not only decoratively but functionally. Latches are used to keep the lids or doors on stained glass structures closed. Hasps are also used to hold the lids of boxes down. In this section, I will show you how to build a tube and rod latch, a rod and pin latch, and a hasp latch.

Latches

The tube and rod latch, shown in Figure IX-9, is used to hold a single door closed or a lid or door which opens from top to bottom closed. I begin construction of the latch by cutting three 1/2″ pieces of brass tube. Refer to Chapter 2 for types of tubing.

The size of the tubing is determined by the weight of the lid or door which it must keep closed. The tubing must be large enough to allow you to use a rod which fits loosely within it. This is usually accomplished by selecting a rod that is one size smaller than the size that you use in hinging. That is, you select a rod that is one size smaller than a rod which fits snugly within the tube. The rod must, however, be strong enough to hold the door or lid without bending out of shape. Be sure to use a wider foil on the edges of the glass where the latch pieces are attached. The strength of the latch greatly depends on the

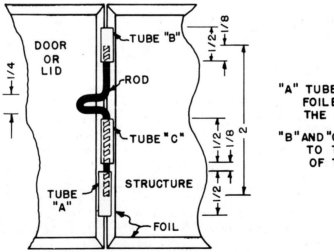

"A" TUBE IS ATTACHED TO THE
    FOILED OUTER SURFACE OF
    THE DOOR OR LID

"B" AND "C" TUBES ARE ATTACHED
    TO THE FOILED OUTER SURFACE
    OF THE STRUCTURE

Figure IX-9   Tube and Rod Latch

42

strength of the bead to which it is attached. Refer to Figure IX-9 for the placement of the pieces on the structure. The total length of a finished latch is about $2^{1}/2$". The pieces should be positioned so that the latch will be in the center of the structure.

Figure IX-10 shows placement of a tube on the edge of a panel. Figure IX-9 shows positioning of the three tubes ("A", "B", and "C") on the lid or door and structure. The "A" piece of tube is lightly tacked to the outside corner of the edge of the door or lid panel.

Figure IX-10   Tube Placement on Panel

The "C" tube is attached to the outside corner edge of the structure panel so that it is directly above, but not touching the tube on the door or lid (about $1/8$" works well), when the door or lid is closed. This will allow the door or lid to be freely opened.

You must now cut a piece of brass rod approximately 4" long. The rod is bent to the specifications shown in Figure IX-11. The long end may be trimmed after fitting if necessary. Measure in $7/8$" from one end and make a 90 degree bend. Approximately $1/4$" after the first bend, double the rod back against itself. After approximately $1/4$", again make a 90 degree bend, making sure that the long leg is a continuance of the line started by the $7/8$" leg.

Figure IX-11   Latch Rod Specifications

Insert the $7/8$" leg into the two pieces of the tube already attached to your structure ("A" and "C"). Make sure that the rod moves freely through the tubes. This rod should pass through the "C" tube first and then extend into the "A" tube. The long leg of the rod should run straight along the space between the door or lid and the structure. Make any adjustments necessary.

Slide the last $1/2$" tube ("B") over the long leg of the rod. The positioning of this tube is critical; refer to Figure IX-9. The tube is positioned so that when the bent portion of the rod is pulled up away from the "A" and "C" tubes already tacked in place, the short end of the rod comes out of the "A" tube, yet remains in the "C" tube. Tack the "B" tube onto the outside corner edge of the structure at a position which will allow the rod to be out of the "A" tube but still within the "C" tube.

This will allow the door or lid to swing open. To close and latch the door or lid, you simply lift the quarter inch tab of the rod (pull away from the "C" and "A" tubes), close the door or lid and slide the tab back towards the "A" tube. The door or lid should now be latched closed. Once you have done this a couple of time and are satisfied with the alignment of all pieces, you may final bead the unit.

Take great care to bead all pieces of the tube well, as this gives the unit strength. Great care must be taken not to get any solder on the moving parts of the latch or inside the tube.

The second latch, the rod and pin latch, is used to keep two doors closed and together. It is shown in Figure IX-12. It can also be used in lieu of the tube and rod latch described earlier in doors which open in the traditional manner, but not on doors which open from top to bottom. This latch does not hold the doors as securely closed as these, but is more decorative and requires less engineering.

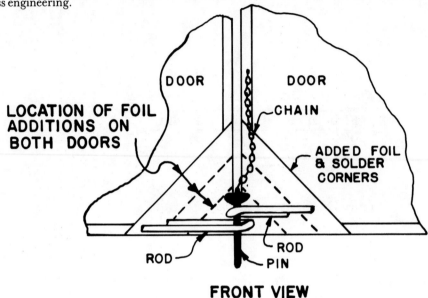

FRONT VIEW

Figure IX-12   Rod and Pin Latch for Double Door

This first thing to do is add some pieces of foil diagonally across the corners where the latch is to be attached. Usually, three strips of ¼" foil are sufficient. The total width at the widest point should be about three quarters of an inch (³/₄"). You may also want to add them to the back of the door panels for aesthetic purposes. Lightly solder them into place. Do not heavily bead these, as you will be soldering to them soon. See Figure IX-12 for location. Cut two pieces of brass rod about one and one-half (1½") inches long.

Take one piece of rod and place one end between the jaws of needlenose pliers and bend the long end around one jaw until it meets the first end, forming a small loop with a long tail; see Figures IX-13 and IX-14 views of finished loops. Be sure to make the loop large enough to allow the latch pin to easily pass through it. Repeat the procedure with the second piece of rod.

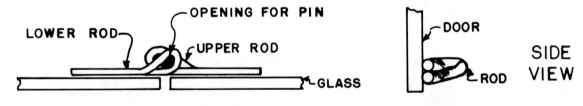

Figure IX-13   Bottom View of Doors   Figure IX-14   Side View of Door

You now should have two identical loops with tails. Position the first loop along the bottom edge of the corner of the door, extending the loop portion past the edge of the door, as shown in Figure IX-13. You will have to trim the end of the tail if it extends beyond the foil added to the corner. The loop should be positioned so that the center of it is in line with the center of the space between the two doors. When positioned, tack in place. The second loop is positioned in the same manner on the second door but slightly above the bottom edge of the door, allowing for the loop to fit just above the loop on the other door. Make sure that the holes in the loop are in line with each other. When you are satisfied with the alignment, tack the loop in place. You may now bead the corners and loops. Great care should be taken to slowly bead this area, as you are working on foil over glass and overheating a large area could cause a crack.

A small amount of solder may be added to the loop to close the point where the end of the loop meets itself. A latch pin must now be made. Cut a piece of brass rod one-half inch (½") long. A ball of solder is now added to one end of the rod. This is done by holding one end of the rod with pliers and placing the other end down against the work surface in a perpendicular position as shown in Figure IX-15. Add a couple of drops of solder against the bottom end of the rod. Heat it and allow it to run around the entire end of the rod. Remove the iron and hold the rod until the solder cools.

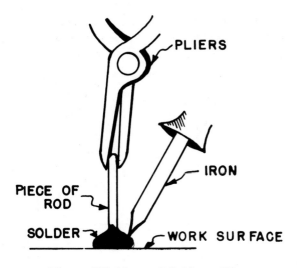

Figure IX-15   Making a Pin

You now should have a pin resembling a round-headed nail. This pin may be used attached or unattached to the structure. I prefer to attach them as they then cannot be lost. This is done by carefully tacking a one and one-half inch (1½") piece of lightweight chain to the large end of the pin at the top of the solder blob, then attach the other end to the edge of one of the doors in such a manner as to allow the easy placement and removal of the pin.

This type of latch is not used on any of the patterns included in this book, but may be useful in future projects.

Hasps

The hasp that I prefer to use resembles the old treasure chest type, through which a padlock can be passed. I secure it with a loop of brass rod. For the construction and placement of pieces, Refer to Figure IX-16. Begin by cutting two pieces of brass tubing three-quarters (¾") of an inch in length. Cut three pieces of brass rod next; one piece three inches long (3"), to be used as the movable loop, the second piece cut at one and one-quarter inches (1¼"). This is for the stationary loop. The third, if used, is for the loop to secure the hasp and is cut approximately one inch long.

When these pieces are cut, you are ready to begin. The first thing you must do is to add a triangular patch of foil to the center top area of the front panel of the box. This is done by adding strips of foil in a diagonal pattern, down from the edge of the box, as shown in Figure IX-16. Be sure that your glass is clean so that the foil will stick. Trim the foil patch with a razor, knife, or blade, to form a triangle pointing downward. Lightly solder coat these pieces and attach them to the top edge of the box.

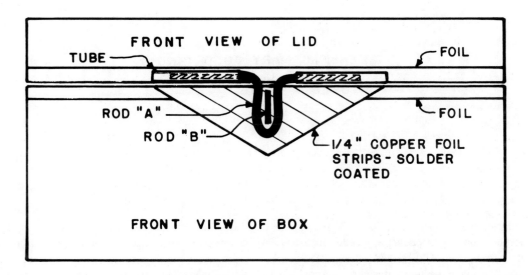

Figure IX-16   Front View of Hasp

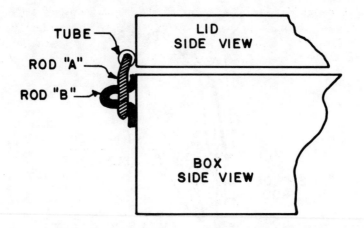

Figure IX-17   End View of Hasp

Now take the one and one-quarter inch (1¼") piece of rod and bed it into the shape shown as Rod "B", Figure IX-17, by doing the following. After one-quarter inch (¼"), again bend the rod 180 degrees back in the direction from which it came. Be sure to leave a space of one-eighth inch (⅛") between the two pieces of rod. After approximately one-quarter inch (¼"), bend the rod another 90 degree angle. The long leg should now be running in line with the one-eighth inch (⅛") leg, as shown in Figure IX-18.

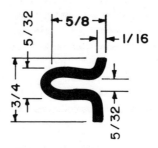

DIMENSIONS VARY ACCORDING
TO THE SIZE OF THE
TUBES & RODS

Figure IX-18   Rod "B", Side View

Trim the long leg to three-eights of an inch (⅜"), if necessary. Attach this loop to the triangular patch on the front of the box. The short leg should be placed at the top edge of the box, with the remainder of the loop running downward along the centerline of the front panel of the box.

You now can final solder the loop to the patch. Do not build the solder up too much, as it might interfere with the movable loop to be added next. Be sure that the patch is strongly attached to the top edge of the box.

Now take the three inch piece of rod. Measure in one-half of an inch (¹/₂″) and make a 90 degree bend. After one-half of an inch (¹/₂), bend the rod 180 degrees back in the direction from which it came. Be sure to leave a space of one-eighth of an inch (¹/₈″) between the two pieces of rod. After approximately one-half of an inch (¹/₂″), make another 90 degree bend. This should make the leg run in line with the first one-half of an inch (¹/₂″) leg, as shown in Figure IX-19. Trim the last leg to a length of ³/₄ inch.

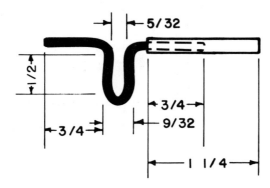

Figure IX-19   Rod "A" and Tube, Front View

Take the two three-quarterinch pieces of tubing and place them over the ends of the loop that you have just made. Move them inward until they are against the two 90 degree bends. With the lid of the box closed, hold the assembly along the bottom outside edge of the lid, so that its loop fits over the loop already attached to the front of the box. When everything is aligned, tack the two pieces of tubing in place.

Check to see that you can move this loop up and down easily over the stationary loop on the front of the box, and make any adjustments necessary. Now firmly attach this assembly to the edge of the lid, and final bead. Take care not to get any solder on the moving parts.

Your hasp is now complete. A small decorative lock may now be added, or a small brass clip can be made. I take a one inch piece of brass rod and bend it into a horseshoe configuration, with the ends bent close together, as shown in Figure IX-20. This can be attached by putting one end of the clip through the exposed loop at the front of the box and allowing it to slide until the clip hangs evenly through the loop.

Figure IX-20   Brass Locking Clip

Chains 10

A chain should be added to the finished box to keep the lid from falling back too far and possibly damaging the hinge or breaking the lid. The positioning of the chain often depends n the type of lid and the internal structure of the box.

The chain must be added in such a manner that it does not interfere with the closing of the lid or the position of a tray. I recommend that trays be positioned to the back of the box or on one side of the box. The chain can therefore be attached to one front, vertical, corner seam, as shown in Figure X-1. I attach to the vertical or bottom seam because it is stronger. Attaching to the top edge seam is not recommended, because the foil can lift or tear with prolonged use of the box. It is often difficult to close the lid properly if the chain is attached to the edge seam.

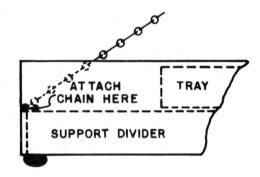

Figure X-1   Chain Installation in a Box with a Tray

The chain is attached to a strong point on the lid in like manner. If you have used a lid with vertical sides or structurally beveled sides, the point of attachment is easy to determine. It should be placed in the front upper corner. If a flat lid is used, try to attach the chain at a seam midway near the side edge of the lid, as shown in Figure X-2. If the lid has no seams, be sure that the bead work around the lid itself is very strong. You should use a wider foil to frame the lid in this case.

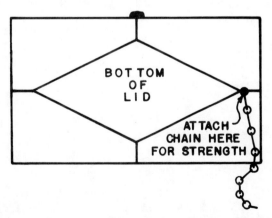

Figure X-2   Chain Installation on Flat Lid

The chain length is determined by measuring from point of attachment in the box to the point of attachment on the lid when it is properly positioned. Then add ¼" to the length to allow for the amount of chain required to attach the chain to the solder beads (⅛" for each end).

The proper position for the lid, when open, is just beyond vertical. This will enable the lid to stand open, not falling forward nor backwards. I have found that the lid stays very well at about 70 degrees to horizontal, as shown in Figure X-3.

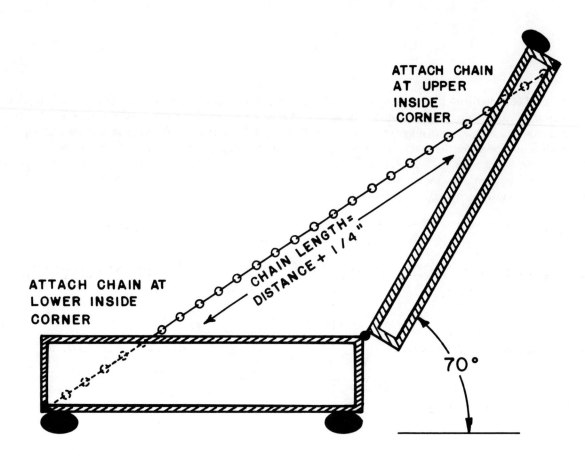

Figure X-3   Typical Chain Installation in a Standard Box

The size of the chain varies according to size and weight of the lid. The clerk at your stained glass supplier will be happy to help you select the proper size for your particular needs.

Knobs, Pulls, and Legs

One of the last creative details that you have to deal with are the knobs, pulls, and legs. These are usually made to coordinate with the lid of the box or its contents. If you have put a shell or cluster of shells into the lid, carefully foil small shells to be used for the "drawer" pull and "lift" knob of the lid. Legs can be made in a half shell design which, when soldered together at the corners, will take on the appearance of a shell, as shown in Figure XI-1.

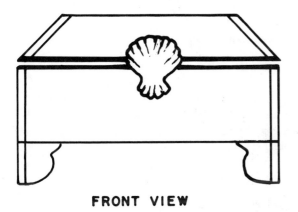
FRONT VIEW

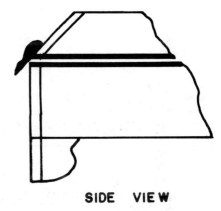
SIDE VIEW

Figure XI-1   Matching Knob and Legs

A diaper pin box might use a large safety pin that has been coated with solder and attached as a lift knob on the lid, as shown in Figure XI-2. Small pins may be solder coated and used as legs.

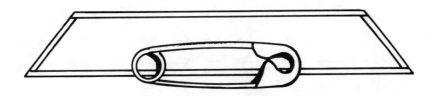

Figure XI-2   Diaper Pin Box Knob

The perfect accents for a recipe box can be made in the shape of a spoon or crossed spoons. This shape can be achieved by carefully shaping 16gauge copper wire with needlenose pliers and filling the shapes with solder, then carefully attaching them to the appropriate places on the box, as shown in Figure XI-3. Be sure to add enough solder to make them strong enough to lift a lid or pull a drawer.

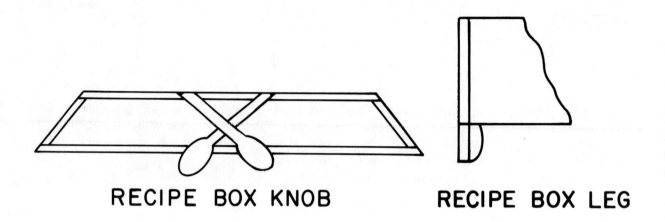

RECIPE BOX KNOB   RECIPE BOX LEG

Figure XI-3   Recipe Box Knob and Leg

Legs can be made in the same manner or might be made of glass to the shape of quarter-circles, which, when joined together at the corner, will look like half a spoon. The lid of the box may be done in a specific motif, such as butterflies, as shown in Figure XI-4, hearts, or flowers, as shown in Figure XI-5. You can create beautiful knobs and pulls by shaping 16 gauge copper wire with needlenose pliers into the appropriate shape and filling in with solder.

Figure XI-4   Butterfly Cutout Knob

Figure XI-5   Flower Cutout Knob

Knobs and pulls should be carefully and firmly attached to the appropriate places on the box. They can carefully be reinforced from the back with a little extra solder if they are attached at an angle. This is the best method of mounting because they are easier to grip if they are mounted at a slight angle to the box, as shown in Figure XI-6.

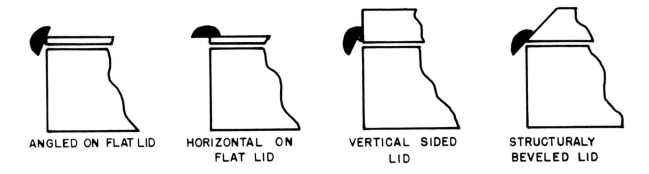

ANGLED ON FLAT LID   HORIZONTAL ON FLAT LID   VERTICAL SIDED LID   STRUCTURALY BEVELED LID

Figure XI-6   Knob Placement on Lids

Polished stones, jewels, or small shaped pieces of glass can also be foiled and used in the same manner. If you look through a hardware or hobby store, you can often find many small brass knobs which can be soldered to the box and used as knobs, pulls, and legs. Many glass suppliers are now stocking small legs, knobs, and pulls which can be added to your box. These may remain brass color, or may be lightly tinned to maintain the same finish as the rest of the soldering on the box.

On a box with a drawer, a knob must be added to the front of the drawer. This will enable you to easily pull the drawer out. I recommend using the same style knob as used to lift the lid.

It is important that this knob be mounted in such a manner that it will be easy to grasp. It must also be attached securely to the front of the drawer. I have found that with time, many drawer pull knobs will work loose if not securely attached. It does not prove sufficient to simply solder it to the outside upper edge of the drawer.

I have found that the most efficient manner is to add a strip of foil down the front center of the drawer, as shown in Figure XI-7. This strip is securely soldered to the top and bottom bead on the drawer. You may want to apply additional solder in a decorative manner to the strip. The pull knob is securely soldered to the upper portion of this strip. Additional solder may be added at the upper back of the knob where it attaches to the strip. Remember to leave enough of the knob extended to easily grasp.

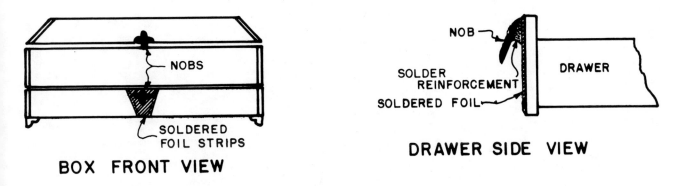

BOX FRONT VIEW   DRAWER SIDE VIEW

Figure XI-7   Drawer Pull Knob Placement

Boxes of Another Shape 12

Introduction

Designing non-square or rectangular boxes requires the use of the same basic principles used in the preceding chapters. The key is always to measure and cut accurately. I will discuss two basic categories in the following section: boxes with many vertical sides and boxes with angular sides.

Before I begin discussion of the boxes, I should discuss a tool that makes their design easy. The adjustable triangle enables the craftsman to draw consistent, like angles. This triangle has an adjustable side which can be set at any angle you choose to work with, and it also has a built-in protractor.

A protractor is another tool that you can use instead of an adjustable triangle. The protractor is a half-round piece of plastic that has markings on it. It will enable you to draw specific angles. These tools are available at most large stationary stores or art and drafting supply stores.

Multisided Boxes

The first thing to determine for a vertical, multisided box is the number of sides that you want. Once you know the number of sides, you must calculate the angle that you will be working with. Since there are 360 degrees in a circle, you simply divide the number of desired sides into 360. If you want an eight sided box, simply divide 360 by 8; the answer is 45. The angle that you use in the design of an eight sided (octagonal) box is therefore 45 degrees. Figure XII-1 gives you the most common angles used to achieve boxes of popular design.

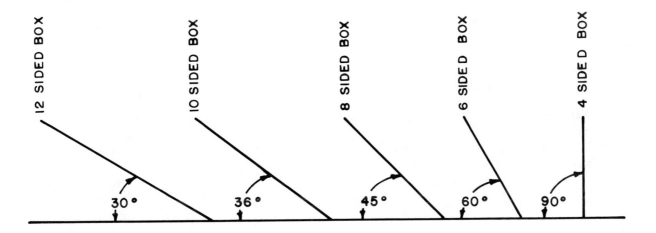

Figure XII-1   Common Angles Used in Box Design

Once the number of sides and the angle have been determined, you must determine how large you want the box. The diameter of the box is a function of the number and the size of the side panels. Figure XII-2 shows the width of each panel required for a predetermined number of panels to arrive at a desired diameter. For example, if you want to build a box that is six inches in diameter and want it to have eight sides, then the width of each panel must be 2¹/₄ inches.

I have compiled the following chart, shown as Figure XII-2, which will give you the most common shapes and diameters that you would work with.

Width in inches of each panel to achieve diameter for number of sides

Diameter/ in inches / No. of Sides	4	5	6	8	10	12
2	$1^3/_4$	$1^7/_{32}$	$^{31}/_{32}$	$^{11}/_{16}$	$^{19}/_{32}$	$^{15}/_{32}$
3	$2^3/_4$	2	$1^{19}/_{32}$	$1^1/_{16}$	$^7/_8$	$^{23}/_{32}$
4	$3^3/_4$	$2^{11}/_{16}$	$2^1/_8$	$1^{15}/_{32}$	$1^7/_{32}$	1
5	$4^3/_4$	$3^{13}/_{32}$	$2^{23}/_{32}$	$1^{27}/_{32}$	$1^{17}/_{32}$	$1^1/_4$
6	$5^3/_4$	$4^5/_{32}$	$3^9/_{32}$	$2^1/_4$	$1^{27}/_{32}$	$1^{17}/_{32}$
7	$6^3/_4$	$4^7/_8$	$3^7/_8$	$2^5/_8$	$2^5/_{32}$	$1^{25}/_{32}$
8	$7^3/_4$	$5^{19}/_{32}$	$4^7/_{16}$	3	$2^{15}/_{32}$	$2^1/_{16}$
9	$8^3/_4$	$6^5/_{16}$	$5^1/_{32}$	$3^{13}/_{32}$	$2^{13}/_{16}$	$2^5/_{16}$
10	$9^3/_4$	$7^1/_{32}$	$5^{19}/_{32}$	$3^{27}/_{32}$	$3^1/_8$	$2^{19}/_{32}$
11	$10^3/_4$	$7^{25}/_{32}$	$6^3/_{16}$	$4^3/_{16}$	$3^{15}/_{32}$	$2^{27}/_{32}$
12	$11^3/_4$	$8^{17}/_{32}$	$6^3/_4$	$4^9/_{16}$	$3^{25}/_{32}$	$3^3/_{32}$
13	$12^3/_4$	$9^7/_{32}$	$7^{11}/_{32}$	$4^{31}/_{32}$	$4^1/_8$	$3^3/_8$
14	$13^3/_4$	$9^{31}/_{32}$	$7^{15}/_{16}$	$5^3/_8$	$4^7/_{16}$	$3^{21}/_{32}$

Figure XII-2   Panel Widths for Standard Diameters

The dimensions in this chart are calculated to give you the outside diameter of a finished structure (plus/minus $^1/_8$"). They are calculated allowing for the use of double strength glass ($^1/_8$"). To design a box of a given diameter (plus/minus $^1/_8$"), refer to the above table to determine the panel width according to the number of sides that you desire in the structure. The height of the panel is up to you. Remember to consider the internal structure of the box when determining the height of the panel. The panel width is determined by selecting the diameter of the structure that you want to make, then following across the dimensions until you come to the desired number of sides.

Example: A 13" diameter box with 8 sides would use 8 panels $4^{31}/_{32}$" wide.

A 6" diameter box with 12 sides would use 12 panels $1^{17}/_{32}$" wide.

A 9" diameter box with 5 sides would use 5 panels $6^5/_{16}$" wide.

Use this information in conjunction with additional information given in this chapter to make a drawing of what will be the bottom panel of the box.

The following is a three step procedure for drawing a typical pattern for the bottom of a multisided box. You will notice that this method utilizes the information that could be obtained from the preceding charts. For the purpose of illustration I have chosen to design a box with eight sides using the panel width of two inches. This should give us a box with a finished diameter of $5^1/_{16}$".

Figure XII-3A shows step one. Draw a straight horizontal line across the bottom of your paper. At the center of that line, a second line up at 90 degrees. Measure 1" in from either side of the vertical line and mark a reference point.

Figure XII-3B shows step two. From one reference point on the horizontal line, draw a line up and away at a 45 degree angle. Measure up this line 2" and mark.

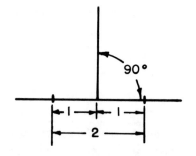

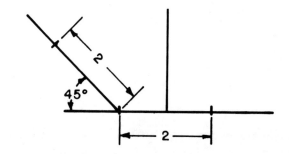

Figure XII-3a   Step One of Pattern Design   Figure XII-3b   Step Two of Pattern Design

Figure XII-3C shows step three. Draw another line up from this point at 45 degrees. Again measure 2" and mark. Continue drawing lines at 45 degrees to each other and measuring 2". These lines should wrap around and meet the first horizontal line at a point 1" from the vertical line that you drew in Step 1. Check that all opposite lines are the same distance from each other.

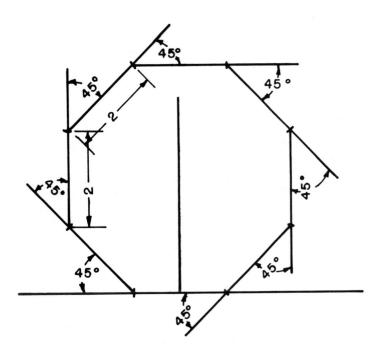

Figure XII-3c   Step Three of Pattern Design

Your finished drawing should look like the one shown in Figure XII-4. This octagon becomes the pattern for the bottom of the box. As you can see, the sides of the box will be 2" wide. The height of these panels will be up to you.

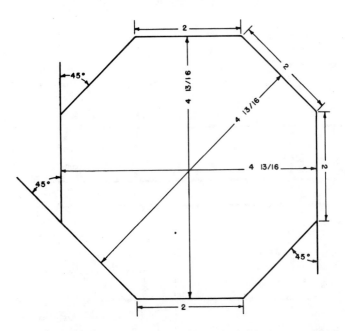

Figure XII-4   Typical Octagon Pattern - 2" Sides

The calculations for a 6, 10, or 12 sided box are done in the same manner only using the appropriate angle. See Figure XII-1 for angles.

Patterning for the top of a multisided box is done in the same manner as with four sided boxes. See section on lids for further explanation of lid styles. With this style of box I recommend using a flat style or vertical sided style lid. All latching, hinging, dividing, and finishing techniques are the same. Even trays and drawers can be added to multisided boxes.

Calculation for the proper angles to be used in the side strips of a structurally beveled lid are quite difficult. If you want to experiment with this style of lid, I will give you a hint that the angle of the cut will increase with the number of sides that your box has. It is advisable to make a couple of cardboard models before you actually begin cutting your glass.

Slope Sided Boxes

Boxes with sloped or non-vertical sides are again somewhat dependent on the craftsman's wishes. You must determine at what angle you want the sides of the box. This angle will change with the number of sides in the box. I cannot give you all of the various angles for all of the different number sides. I will give you some and you can experiment from there.

Figure XII-5 may be used to determine at which angle to cut strips of glass in order to achieve a box with sides sloped at a specific angle to a table top. This table will help to determine these angles on multisided boxes. If, for example, you wanted an eight sided box with sides that sloped towards the table at 40 degrees. The eight side strips would be cut at a 73 degree angle. The height and width of these strips would be determined by the overall size of box that you desire.

No. of Box Sides	Slope of Box Sides					
	30°	35°	40°	45°	50°	90°
16	80°	81°	81.5°	82°	82.5°	90°
14	78.5°	79°	80°	80.5°	81.5°	90°
12	76.5°	77.5°	78°	79°	80°	90°
10	74.5°	75.5°	76.5°	77.5°	78.5°	90°
8	71°	71.5°	73°	73.5°	75°	90°
6	63°	64.5°	66°	67.5°	69.5°	90°

Figure XII-5   Cutting Angles for Slope Sided Boxes

The shape of the side panels of one of these slope sided boxes is referred to in geometry as a trapezoid. A trapezoid is defined as a figure with four sides only two of which are parallel. In the trapezoids that I work with, the other two sides are at the same angles to these parallel lines (see Figure XII-6). The shorter of the parallel lines is used as the bottom edge of the box. The upper edge of the box is the longer parallel line. In box lids which use trapezoids as side panels the longer line represents the bottom edge of the lid.

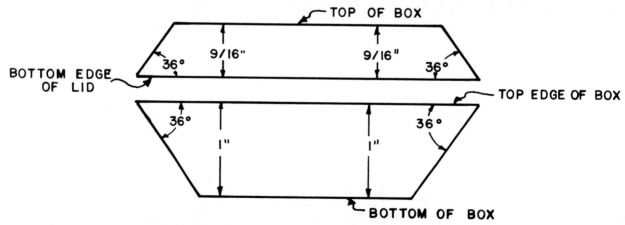

Figure XII-6   Trapezoidal Box and Lid Sides

Dividing these boxes is done in the same manner as in vertical sided boxes. The ends of the divider panels are cut at the same angle as the finished outside angle of the side panel of the box, not the angle of the panel itself (see Figure XII-7).

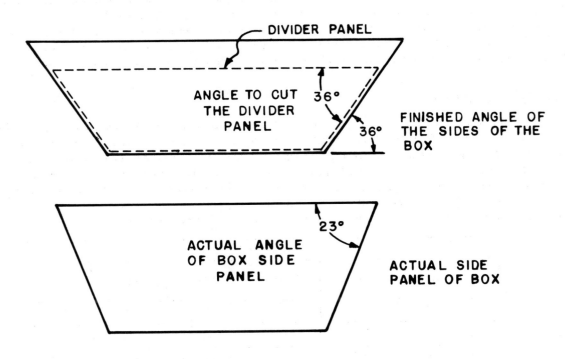

Figure XII-7   Divider Panels in Boxes with Angled Sides

Drawers are not recommended in this style box. Trays may be made but require a lot of engineering. If you choose to try, remember that you can begin by using the same angles as in the sides, themselves.

Lids for boxes with angular sides should be either flat or angular (structurally beveled). The angles used in the lid should be the same as those used in the box itself. This creates a much more pleasing effect.

All hinging and finishing of boxes of another shape are done in the same manner as standard rectangular boxes. Some special circumstances may arise when modifications will best be made. The section on hinges should help you figure them out.

As you have probably realized, almost anything is possible with stained glass. Boxes offer a unique chance to be very expressive and ingenious. You can make about any shape with features if you take the time to think them out. Careful calculations are always necessary to ensure the success of the finished product.

Patterns—General Information

The patterns contained in this book are designed to give you a varied selection of possible box designs. They represent a wide selection of sizes, shapes and difficulties. Most instructions are generalized and designed to be used in conjunction with the text. I strongly recommend that you do not vary the types of glass that are recommended in the specific patterns. With experience, you should be able to make pattern adjustments that will enable you to make such variations.

REMEMBER THAT THE SUCCESS OF A PROJECT WILL DEPEND ON HOW ACCURATELY YOU HAVE FOLLOWED THE PATTERN AND CUT THE GLASS. I have left the design of most of the box lids up to you. Some designs require the use of specific lid styles, which I have included; please follow them. The addition of legs, knobs, latches, etc., is entirely up to you.

General guidelines that should be followed in the construction of boxes are listed below.

1. Always choose your glass carefully, giving special consideration to texture and thickness.
2. When laying out your pattern before cutting, be sure to allow for uniformity in graining on the glass.
3. Remember to choose the proper thickness of glass or correctly figure any compensations which might be necessary to ensure proper fit.
4. When cutting your glass, remember that accuracy is of the utmost importance. The key to putting any geometric structure together successfully is working with accurately cut pieces. Make sure that all angles are sharp and clean. Grind off all spurs.
5. If you are using a glass stripper to cut your box pieces, be sure to make all cuts that will be set at a given dimension before re-setting the stripper. This will insure the proper fit of all pieces.
6. Clean your glass thoroughly and carefully apply the copper foil. Make sure that the foil is firmly pressed to the glass and that the corners are free from wrinkles or bulges.
7. Follow the instructions carefully, step-by-step. They have been designed to help you put your structure together in the easiest and most efficient manner.
8. Remember to be sparing with the flux, as it can damage the mirror used in the box. Don't be afraid to wash and dry your project frequently.
9. When soldering, be sure to thoroughly bead all seams and edges. Be sure to give careful attention to any seams that receive a lot of hand contact or stress from hinges, latches, chains and knobs.
10. Now, after giving you all of these do's and don'ts, I want you to venture forth with these patterns and have fun. Be creative and expressive. Don't be afraid to experiment. Remember that there is nothing that you can't add with careful consideration and compensation.

The legend shown below should be referenced when reading the patterns.

LEGEND

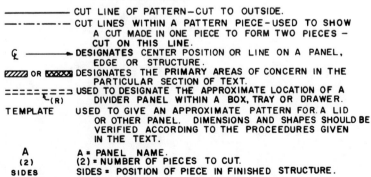

Pattern 1

FINISHED SIZE: 3¹/₄" by 3¹/₄" by 2¹/₄" high.

APPROXIMATE TIME FOR COMPLETION: 1¹/₂ hours.

RECOMMENDED GLASS: ¹/₄ square foot of glass, opalescent or antique for the side "B" panels. (Four 2" by 3" bevels may be substituted.) One 3 by 3 piece of double strength mirror for the "A" panel. One-eight square foot for the "C" panel.

1. Accurately cut and foil all pieces. 2" x 3" bevels may be substituted for the four sides. Cut bottom mirror panel to exact dimensions of the long side of the bevel.

2. Place the bottom panel face up on the work surface. Tack two panels to each other at the joining corners, forming a 90 degree angle. Use the bottom panel as a jig to ensure that the sides remain square. Attach the remaining two sides, one at a time, to each other and to the bottom panel.

3. Follow the techniques in this book to finish solder, patina, and wash the box.

4. Construct the lid according to the pattern or design one yourself. Be sure to treat the lid as a small window pattern, cut to the inside of all lines. If you design your own lid, follow the procedures in the Lid Section of the book for some helpful hints.

5. Finish solder, patina, and wash the lid.

6. Refer to the section on hinging and proceed with the recommended style.

7. Refer to the section on knobs, latches, legs, and chains for the finishing touches that you might desire.

C
(1)

LID TEMPLATE

B
(1)

MIRROR BOTTOM

A
(4)

BOX SIDES

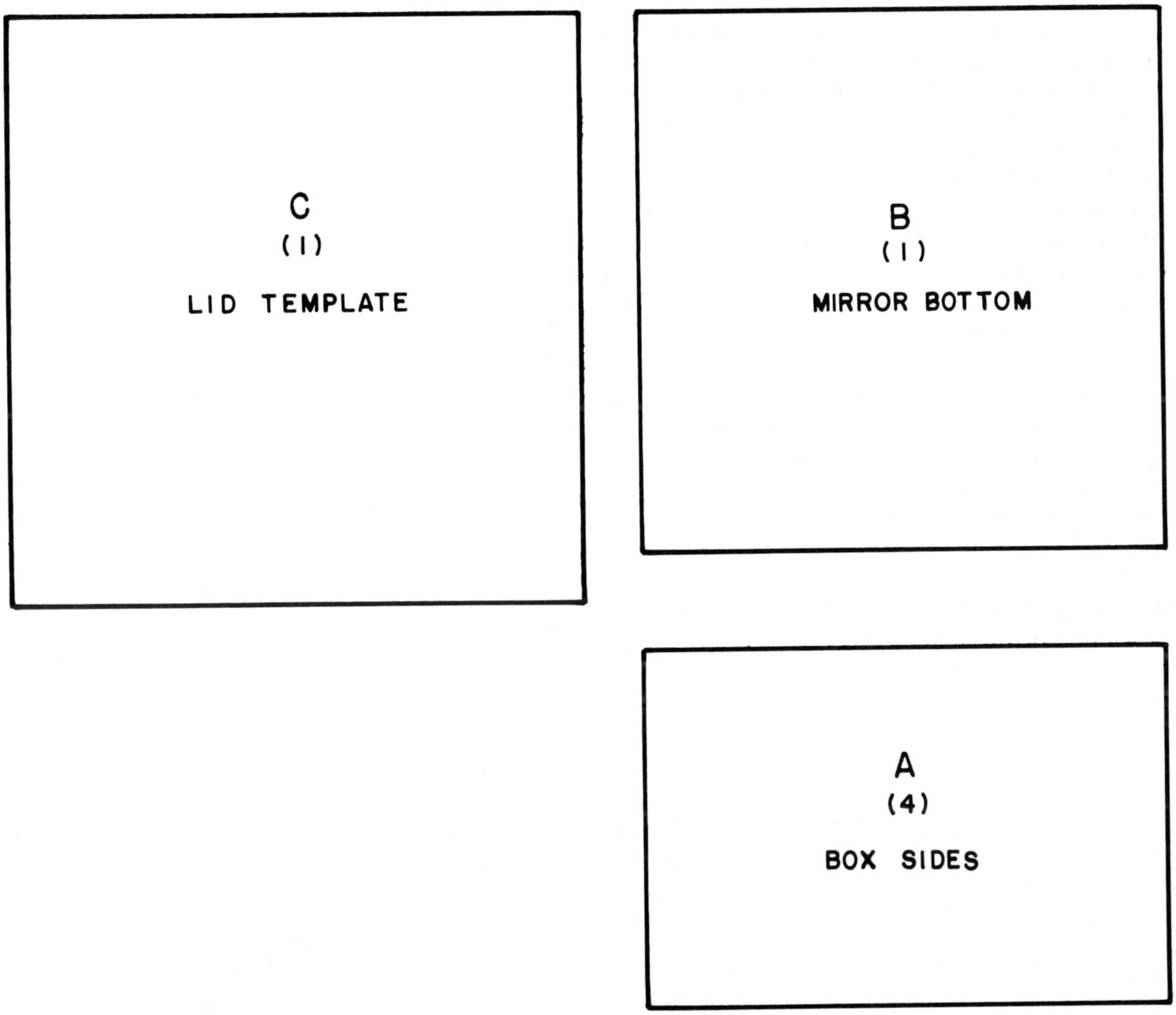

Pattern 2

FINISHED SIZE: 5" x 5" x 2"

APPROXIMATE TIME FOR COMPLETION: 2½ hours.

RECOMMENDED GLASS: ¼ square foot of double strength mirror for panel "A"; ¼ square foot glass of your choice or 2 x 2 bevels for "B" panels. The lid "C" panel requires a total of ¼ square foot of glass. Design is optional.

PROCEDURE:

1. Accurately cut and foil all pieces.
2. Follow the basic box construction chapter for the attachment of the eight sides to the bottom panel.
3. Refer to the section on lids for ideas for the design and construction of a lid for your box.
4. Finish solder, patina, and wash.
5. Refer to appropriate sections on hinges and accents for the box.

B
(8)
SIDES

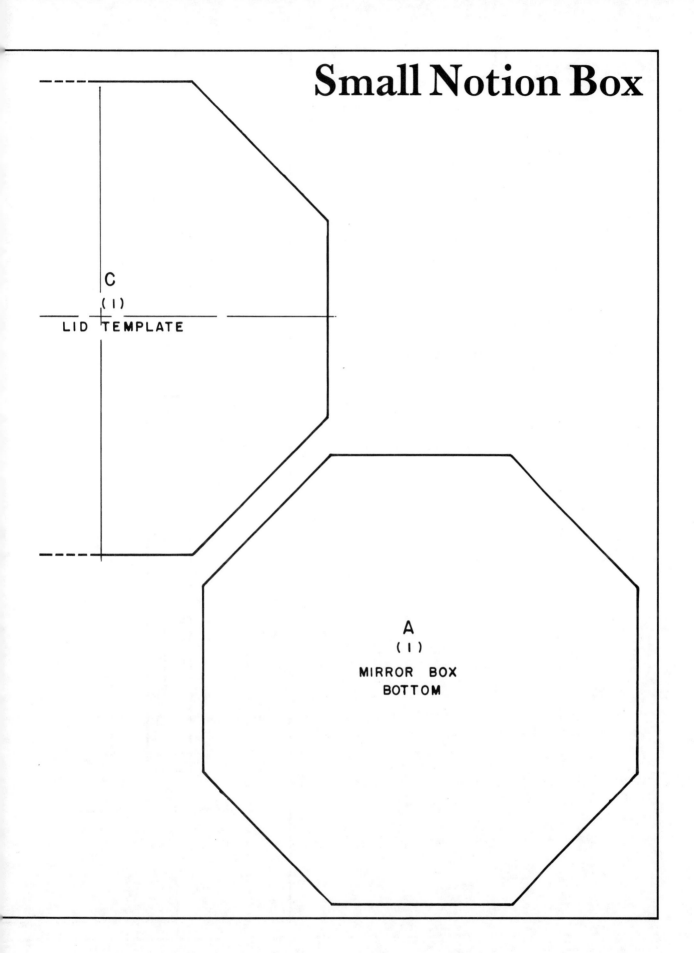

C

(1)

LID TEMPLATE

A

(1)

MIRROR BOX
BOTTOM

Pattern 3

FINISHED SIZE: 6³/₄" x 4³/₄" x 3¹/₂"

APPROXIMATE TIME FOR COMPLETION: Four hours.

RECOMMENDED GLASS: ¹/₂ square foot double strength mirror for panel "A". "B" and "C" panels may be made of the glass of your choice. Bevels 2 x 4 may be substituted for the "B" panels, and 2 x 2 bevels may be substituted for the "C" panels. The lid, "F", requires a total of ¹/₂ square foot of glass. (The amount may vary according to the lid style that you choose.) Panels "E" and "D" provide for a vertical sided lid. Panel "F" is for the center of the vertical sided lid.

PROCEDURE:

1. Accurately cut and foil all pieces.
2. Follow basic box construction procedures to assemble the basic box. If you desire to add a couple of dividers, carefully measure and cut the divider strips according to procedures detailed on the section on compartments.
3. Design and construct the lid of your choice according to the basic pattern pieces. If bevels are used in the box, I recommend using a flat lid.
4. Finish solder patina, and wash according to procedures in the book.
5. Hinge and add finish accents according to the methods prescribed in the book.

E (6)
LID SIDE PANELS

D (2)
LID FRONT AND BACK PANELS

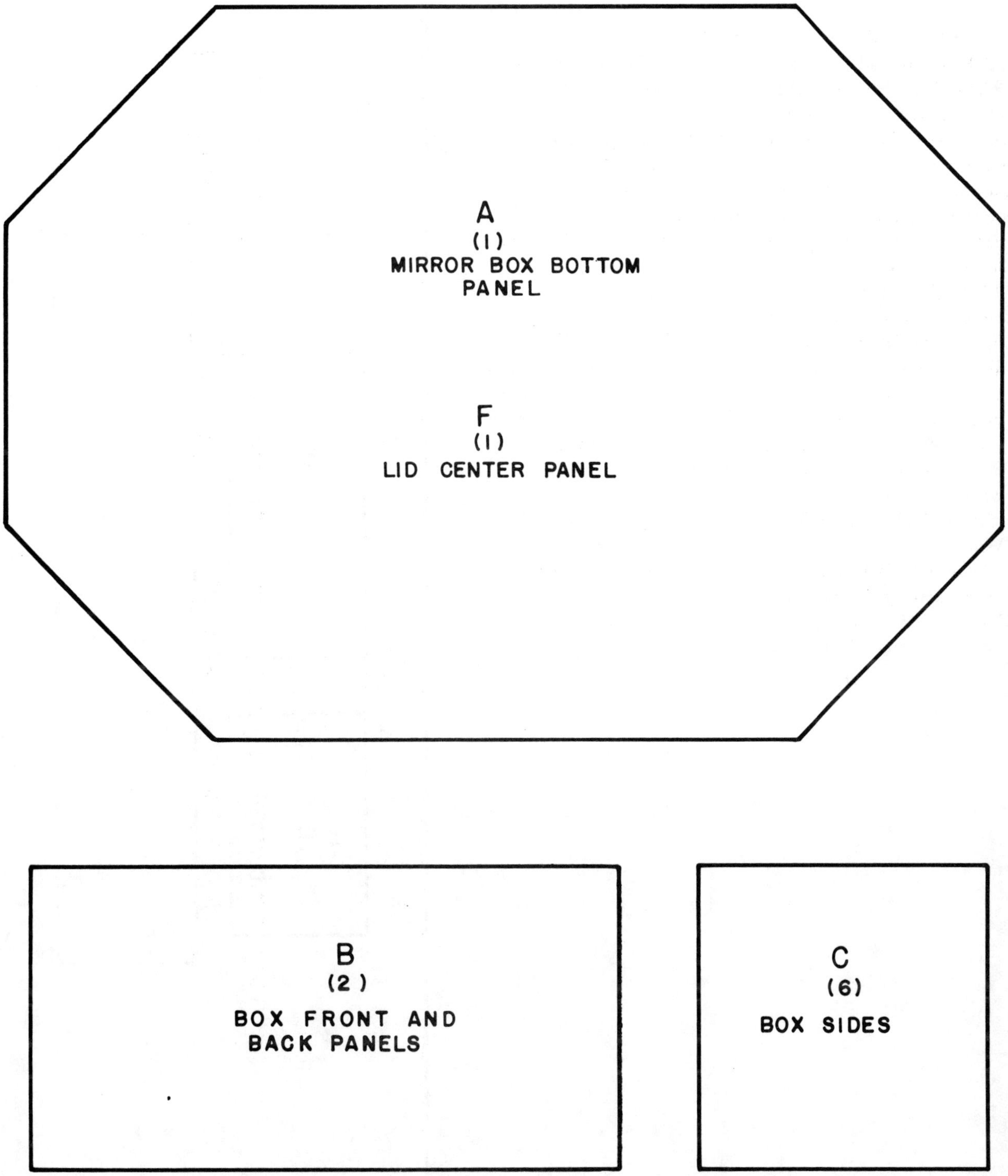

A
(1)
MIRROR BOX BOTTOM
PANEL

F
(1)
LID CENTER PANEL

B
(2)
BOX FRONT AND
BACK PANELS

C
(6)
BOX SIDES

Pattern 4—

FINISHED SIZE: 3¹/₄" x 5¹/₄" x 2¹/₈"

APPROXIMATE TIME FOR COMPLETION: Four hours.

RECOMMENDED GLASS: ¹/₄ square foot double strength mirror for panel "A"; ¹/₂ square foot for "B" and "C" panels in the glass of your choice; ¹/₄ square foot, single strength, clear window glass for dividers, panels "D", "E", and "F". The lid requires approximately ¹/₂ square foot glass, depending on the style that you choose.

PROCEDURE:

1. Cut and foil all box panels, "A", "B", "C", "D", "E", and "F". The lid piece or pieces should be cut after the box has been completed, in order to verify the lid shape, size, and dimensions.
2. Follow the basic box construction procedures outlined in this book. This pattern calls for short dividers to be added to the inside perimeter of this box. The approximate location of the dividers is shown by dashes in Panel "A". "D" and "E" are support dividers for use with a tray. A small tray may be added but is not patterned. The procedures for tray design are in Chapter VI. Remember that when initially constructing this box, do not solder the inside seams, as this will interfere with the addition of the dividers.
3. When the box is completed, verify the lid pattern shape, correct if necessary, and construct the patterned lid or design one of your own following the instructions in Chapter VIII.
4. Hinge, add finishing accents, and clean according the the recommendations made in the book.

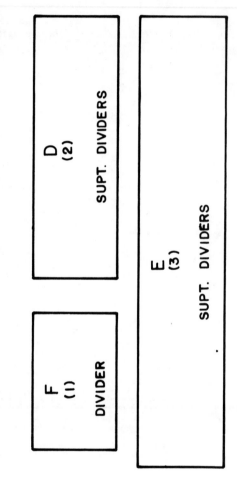

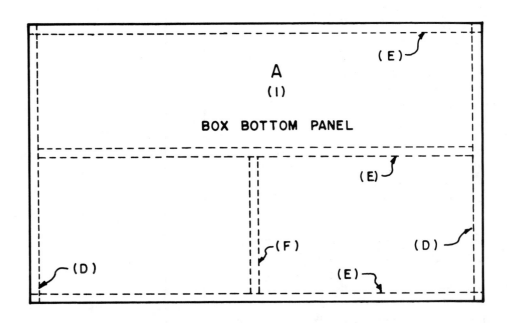

A
(I)

BOX BOTTOM PANEL

(E)

(E)

(F)

(D)

(D)

(E)

B
(2)

FRONT & BACK

C
(2)

SIDES

Pattern 5

FINISHED SIZE: 5¼ x 7¼ x Approximately 3½"

APPROXIMATE TIME FOR COMPLETION: Six hours.

RECOMMENDED GLASS: Panels "A" and "G" ¾ square foot, double strength mirror. Panels "D", "E", "F", "H", "I", "J", and "K", single strength, clear window glass, ½ square foot. Panels "B" and "C" should be opalescent glass, approximately ¾ square foot required. The lid, "L" and "M", requires approximately ½ square foot of glass, depending on the pattern that you select. The pattern provided calls for vertical sides on the lid. The center design is your choice.

PROCEDURE:

1. Accurately cut and foil panels "A" through "J". The remaining panels for the lid should be cut after you have completed the box, and can pattern and make any adjustments necessary to the pattern provided. See Chapter VIII on lids for procedure.

2. Follow the basic box construction procedures outlined in the book. Remember that when initially assembling the main box, do not solder until the dividers have been added.

3. Finish solder, patina, and wash the box and dividers.

4. Tack together the "G" through "J" panels to form the tray. Before final beading, check the tray's fit within the box. Remember, there should be some gap between the tray and the sides of the box; approximately ³⁄₁₆" is advisable. Make any adjustments necessary for proper fit and final bead, patina, and wash.

5. When the box and tray are complete, verify the lid pattern fit. Make any adjustments to the pattern and cut and foil the pieces. Follow construction procedures from the text.

6. Hinge and add finish accents according to the methods prescribed in the book.

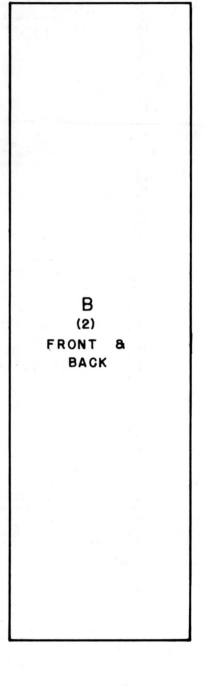

B
(2)
FRONT &
BACK

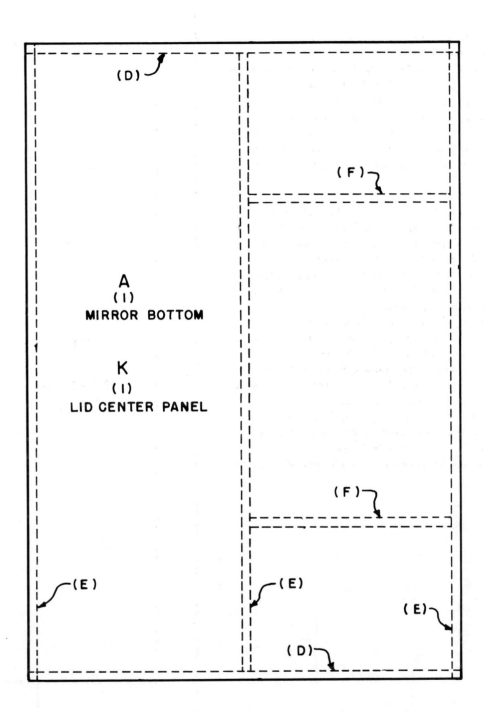

(D)

(F)

A
(I)
MIRROR BOTTOM

K
(I)
LID CENTER PANEL

(F)

(E)

(E)

(E)

(D)

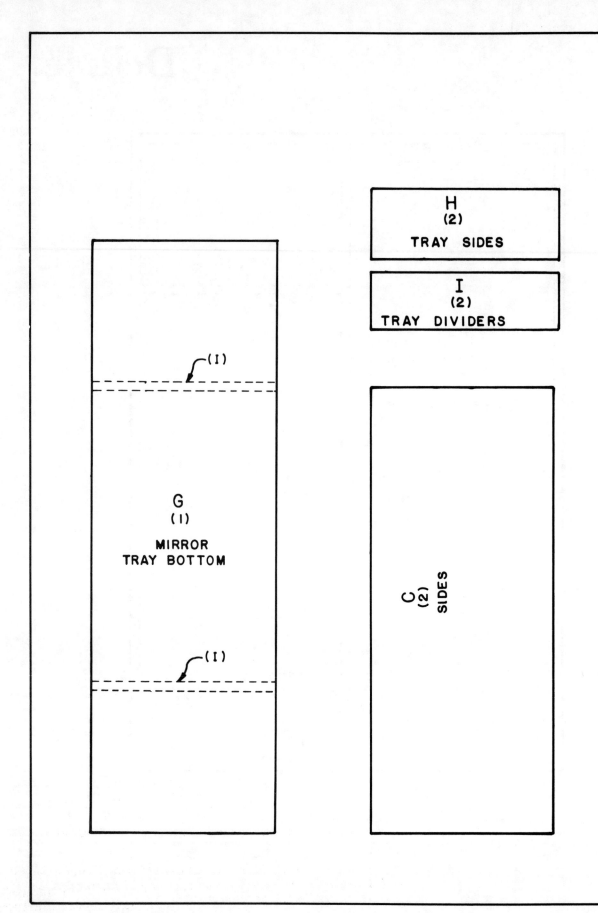

H
(2)
TRAY SIDES

I
(2)
TRAY DIVIDERS

G
(1)
MIRROR
TRAY BOTTOM

(I)

(I)

C
(2)
SIDES

Deluxe

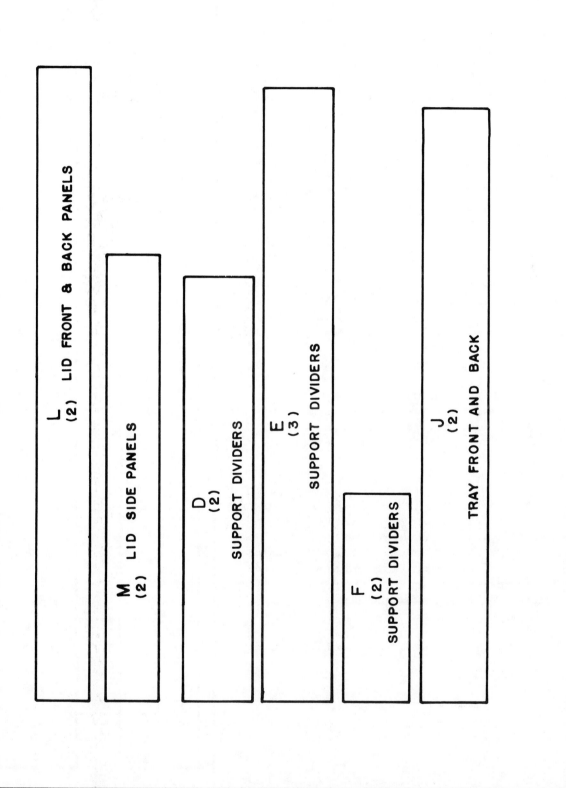

L
(2) LID FRONT & BACK PANELS

M
(2) LID SIDE PANELS

D
(2)
SUPPORT DIVIDERS

E
(3)
SUPPORT DIVIDERS

F
(2)
SUPPORT DIVIDERS

J
(2)
TRAY FRONT AND BACK

Pattern 6

MATERIALS: One pound 50/50 solder, ¼" copper foil (wider may be used for specific effects; see text), flux, brass tube and rod, one inch light chain, patina, miscellaneous material for lid.

FINISHED SIZE: 6¼" x 9¼" x approximately 3¾".

APPROXIMATE TIME FOR COMPLETION: Twelve hours.

RECOMMENDED GLASS: Panels "B", "C", "D", "E", and "V" require 1½ square foot opalescent glass. Panels "F", "L", and "Q" require 2 square feet double strength mirror. Panels "A", "G", "H", "I", "J", "K", "M", "N", "O", "P", "R", "S", "T", and "U" require 2 square feet of single strength, clear window glass. The lid panels require approximately one square foot opalescent glass, according to your lid design and pattern. "X", "Y", and "Z" require approximately one square foot total. However, the top will vary according to the design in panel "Z".

1. Accurately cut and foil panels "B", "C", "D", "E", "A", and "F".

2. Assemble the above pieces, except "E", according to the procedure prescribed in the sections on Compartments, Trays, and Drawers.

3. Accurately cut and foil panels "G", "H", "J", "K", and "I" after verifying their measurements. They may have been altered slightly due to your cutting or assembly of the primary box parts.

4. Install the above pieces in the primary box. Final bead this structure according to the procedures in the book. Wash the entire box, and proceed.

5. Construction of the tray begins by again verifying the measurements of the primary box and making any alterations to the pattern that might be necessary. Accurately cut and foil panels "M", "N", "O", "P", and "L". Assemble according to the section on trays. Final bead and wash.

6. The drawer may now be made. Check the measurements of the drawer opening of the primary box and modify the pattern, if necessary. Cut and foil panels "Q", "S", "R", "U" and "T". Assemble according to the section on trays. Attach panel "E" as drawer front according to text. Finish solder and wash.

7. The lid, "X", "Y", and "Z", may now be constructed according to the pattern or your own design. Be sure to make any alterations to the pattern if necessary.

8. Attach panels "V" as legs. Feel free to design your own legs.

9. Add hinge, knobs, and pulls according to the procedures in the text.

10. Final bead any areas that you might have missed. Patina, wash, and polish.

H
(3)

TRAY SUPPORT DIVIDERS

M
(2)

TRAY FRONT AND BACK

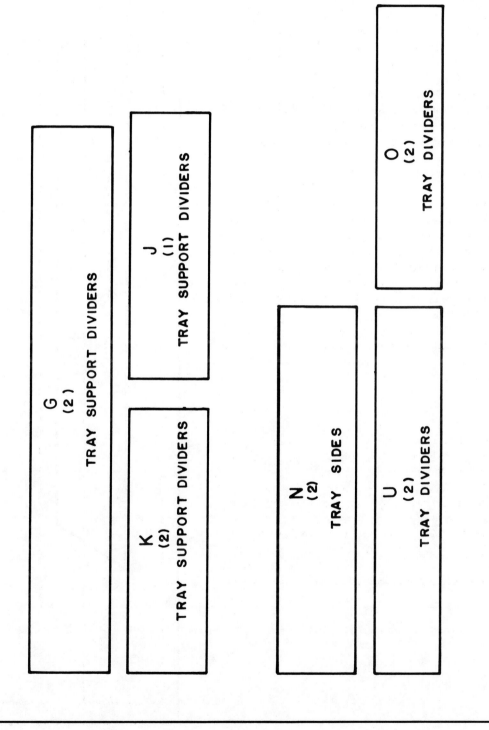

G
(2)
TRAY SUPPORT DIVIDERS

J
(1)
TRAY SUPPORT DIVIDERS

K
(2)
TRAY SUPPORT DIVIDERS

N
(2)
TRAY SIDES

U
(2)
TRAY DIVIDERS

O
(2)
TRAY DIVIDERS

Custom Deluxe Box—List of Parts

LID:
"Z" (1) Lid center panel
"X" (2) Lid side panels
"Y" (2) Lid front and back panels
BOX:
"A" (1) Clear glass bottom
"F" (1) Mirror "false" bottom
"B" (2) Box sides
"C" (1) Box back
"D" (1) Box front
"E" (1) Drawer front
"V" (8) Box legs
BOX DIVIDERS:
"G" (2) Interior side support dividers
"H" (3) Interior front, center and back support dividers
"K" (2) Short support dividers
"J" (1) Short support dividers
TRAY:
"L' (1) Tray bottom (mirror)
"M" (2) Tray front and back
"N" (2) Tray sides
"O" (2) Tray dividers
"U" (2) Tray dividers
DRAWER:
"P" (1) Drawer bottom (mirror)
"Q" (2) Drawer sides
"R" (1) Drawer back
"E" (1) Drawer front
"S" (2) Drawer dividers
"T" (2) Drawer dividers

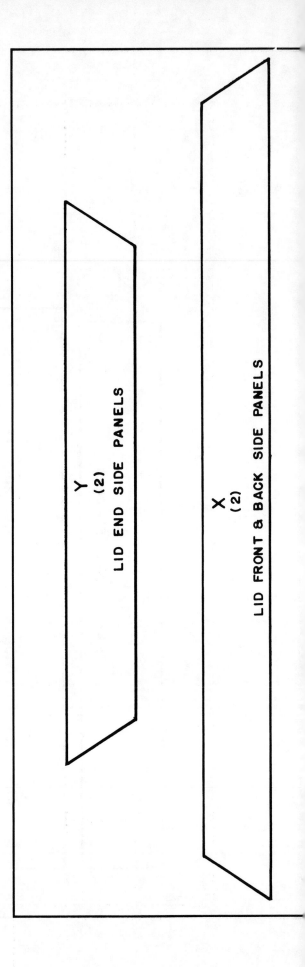

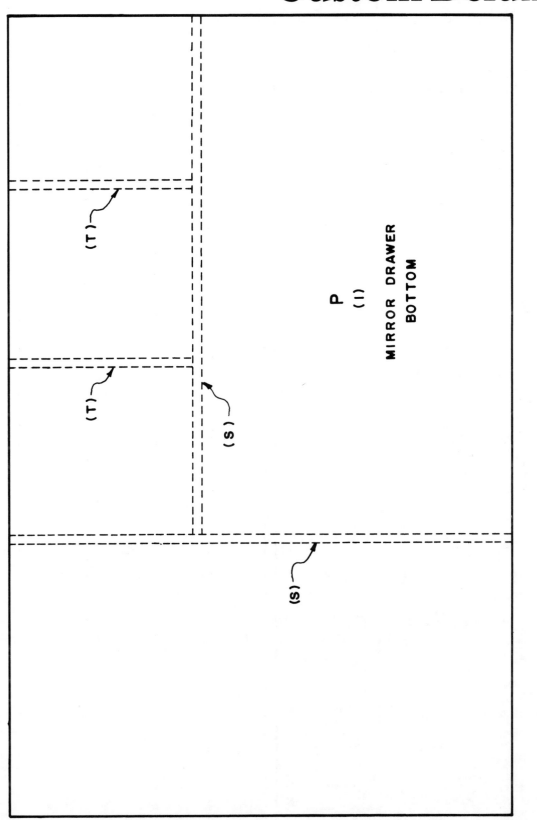

MIRROR DRAWER
BOTTOM

P
(1)

(T)

(T)

(S)

(S)

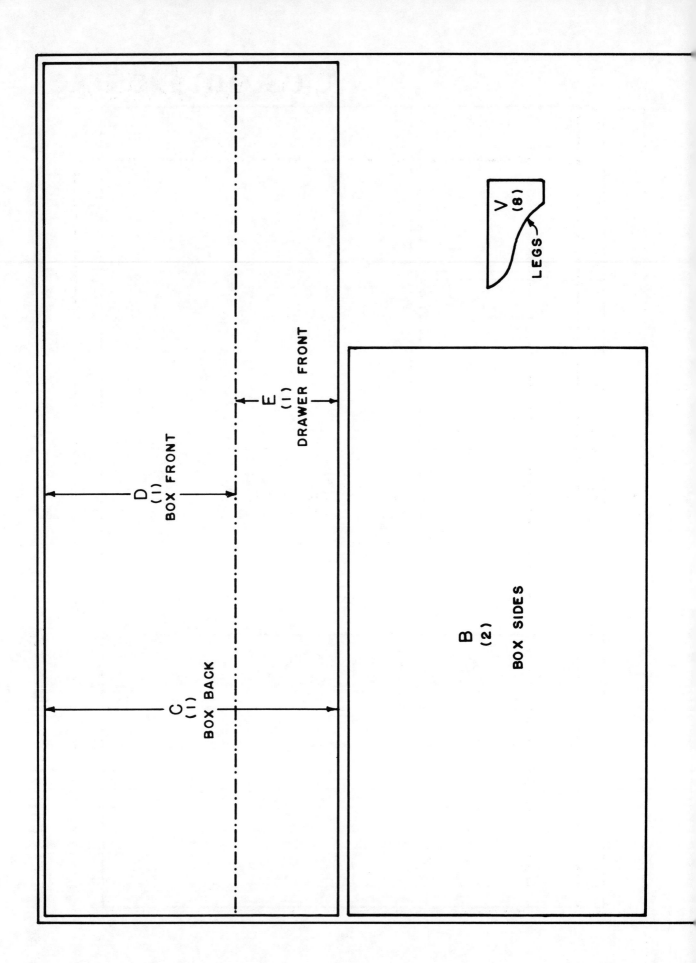

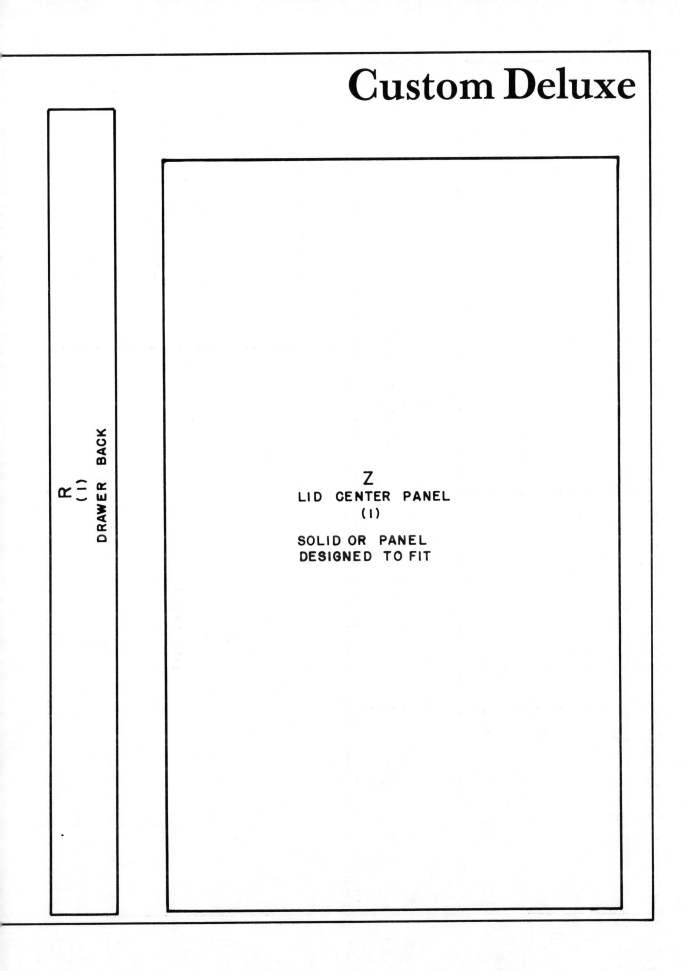

R
(1)
DRAWER BACK

Z
LID CENTER PANEL
(1)

SOLID OR PANEL
DESIGNED TO FIT

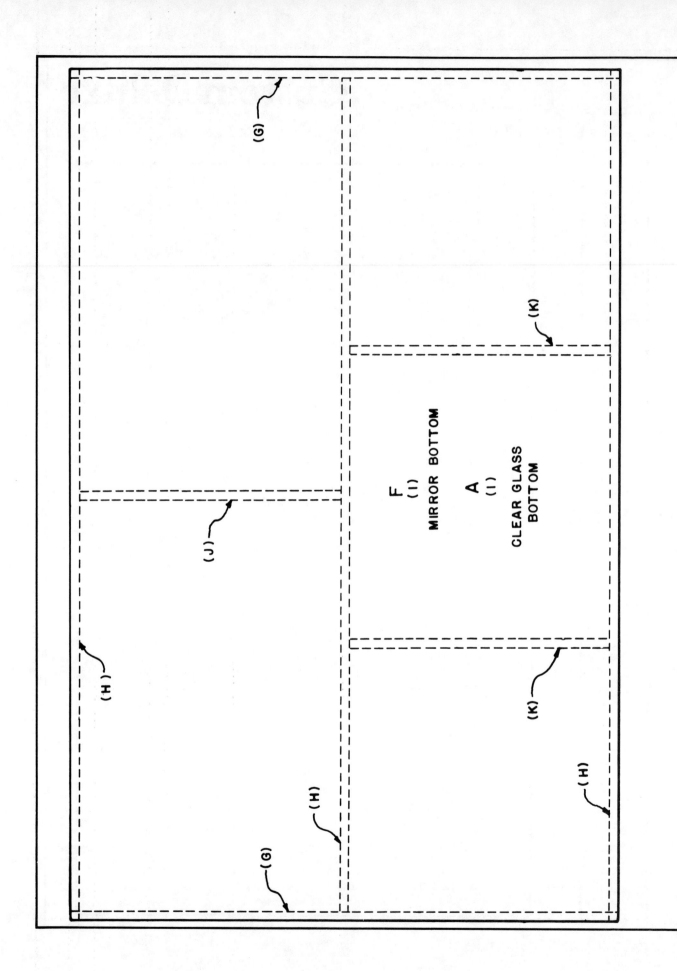

F
(1)
MIRROR BOTTOM

A
(1)
CLEAR GLASS
BOTTOM

(G)

(H)

(J)

(K)

(K)

(H)

(G)

(H)

80

Custom Deluxe

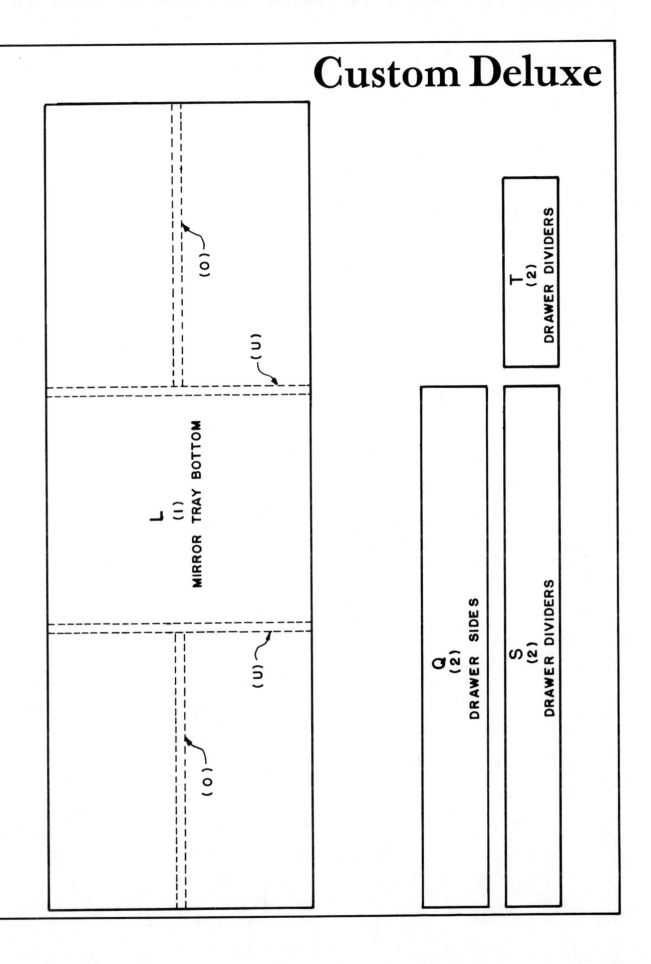

L
(1)
MIRROR TRAY BOTTOM

(O)

(U)

(U)

(O)

T
(2)
DRAWER DIVIDERS

Q
(2)
DRAWER SIDES

S
(2)
DRAWER DIVIDERS

Pattern 7

FINISHED SIZE: 8" round by 2" high.

APPROXIMATE TIME FOR COMPLETION: 4 hours.

RECOMMENDED GLASS: 1 square foot double strength mirror for bottom ("A"). ³/₄ square foot glass of your choice for "C" panels. The lid will use approximately 1 square foot of the glass of your choice for the design that you choose.

PROCEDURE:

1. Accurately cut and foil all "A" and "C" panels.

2. Plae the foiled "A" panel on your clean work surface face up. Solder 2 "C" panels together so that they will remain flat during assembly (these panels will allow you to attach the hinge). Attach these two panels at the bottom of the seam to the mirror, so that the ends are slightly away from the edge of the mirror. Begin tacking the remaining "C" panels, one at a time, around the mirror. You should begin at one side of the two rigid "C" panels and end at the other. If any gap occurs realign a few panels so that the gap is virtually unnoticeable. These panels should be tacked to the mirror and to each other. When you are satisfied with the alignment of all panels final bead the entire structure, patina and thoroughly wash.

3. Invert the box on the "A" pattern and make any alterations necessary to ensure proper fit (it should increase approximately ¹/₈" on all sides). Design the pattern of your choice within this template. Remember to treat this pattern as a window and allow for growth when cutting and assembling, as this will cause the lid not to fit.

4. Hinge, add legs, knobs and chain according to the procedures detailed in the book. Thoroughly wash and polish the entire structure.

C

(32)
SIDES

Memories

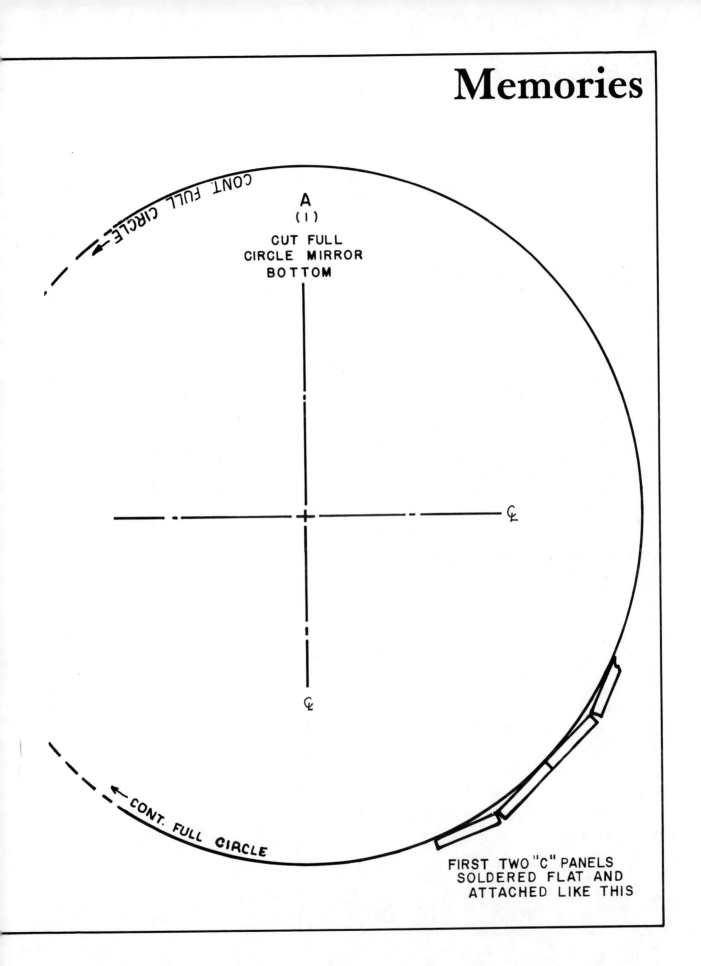

CONT FULL CIRCLE

A
(I)
CUT FULL
CIRCLE MIRROR
BOTTOM

₵

₵

CONT. FULL CIRCLE

FIRST TWO "C" PANELS
SOLDERED FLAT AND
ATTACHED LIKE THIS

Pattern 8

FINISHED SIZE: 5³/₄" x 3¹/₄" x 4" high.

APPROXIMATE TIME FOR COMPLETION: Three hours.

RECOMMENDED GLASS: All glass should be opalescent. Bottom panel "J" need not be in mirror. Panels "A", "B", "C", "D", "E", "F", "G", and "H": one square foot. Panel "I": ¹/₄ square foot. Panel "J": ¹/₄ square foot.

PROCEDURE:

1. Accurately cut and foil all panels (see Step 3).

2. Attach panels "B", "D", "E", and "H" around the "J" bottom panel, according to techniques in the text on basic box construction. Finish solder bead, patina, and thoroughly wash this structure.

3. The "I" panel may be cut as patterned or divided into the design of your choice. Remember to work within the pattern borders. If you have elected to pattern this panel, cut, foil and tack them together to form the finished panel. Lay this panel, face down, on your work surface, and attach the "A", "C", "F", and "G" panels around it. Remember that the "A" panel attaches at what will be the front of the patterned top. Remember also that the "A", "C", and "F" panels must be attached so that they will fit atop the box. Follow construction procedures in tacking these pieces together. When the lid is lightly tacked together, set the lid on the finished box, and make sure that all panels align. Make any adjustments necessary. When you are certain that the lid will align with the box, finish solder the lid. Patina and wash the lid.

4. Hinge and add finishing accents. Wash, patina, and dry.

RECIPE BOX

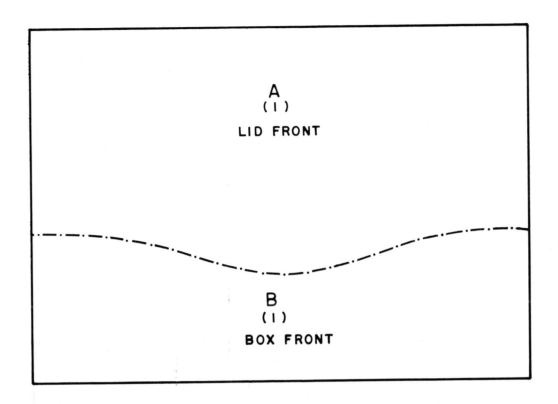

A
(I)
LID FRONT

B
(I)
BOX FRONT

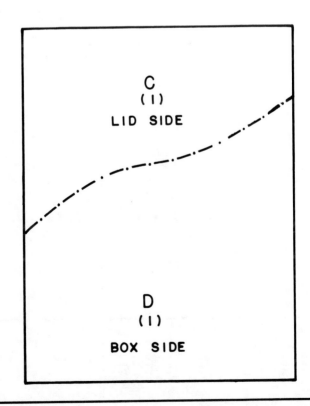

C
(I)
LID SIDE

D
(I)
BOX SIDE

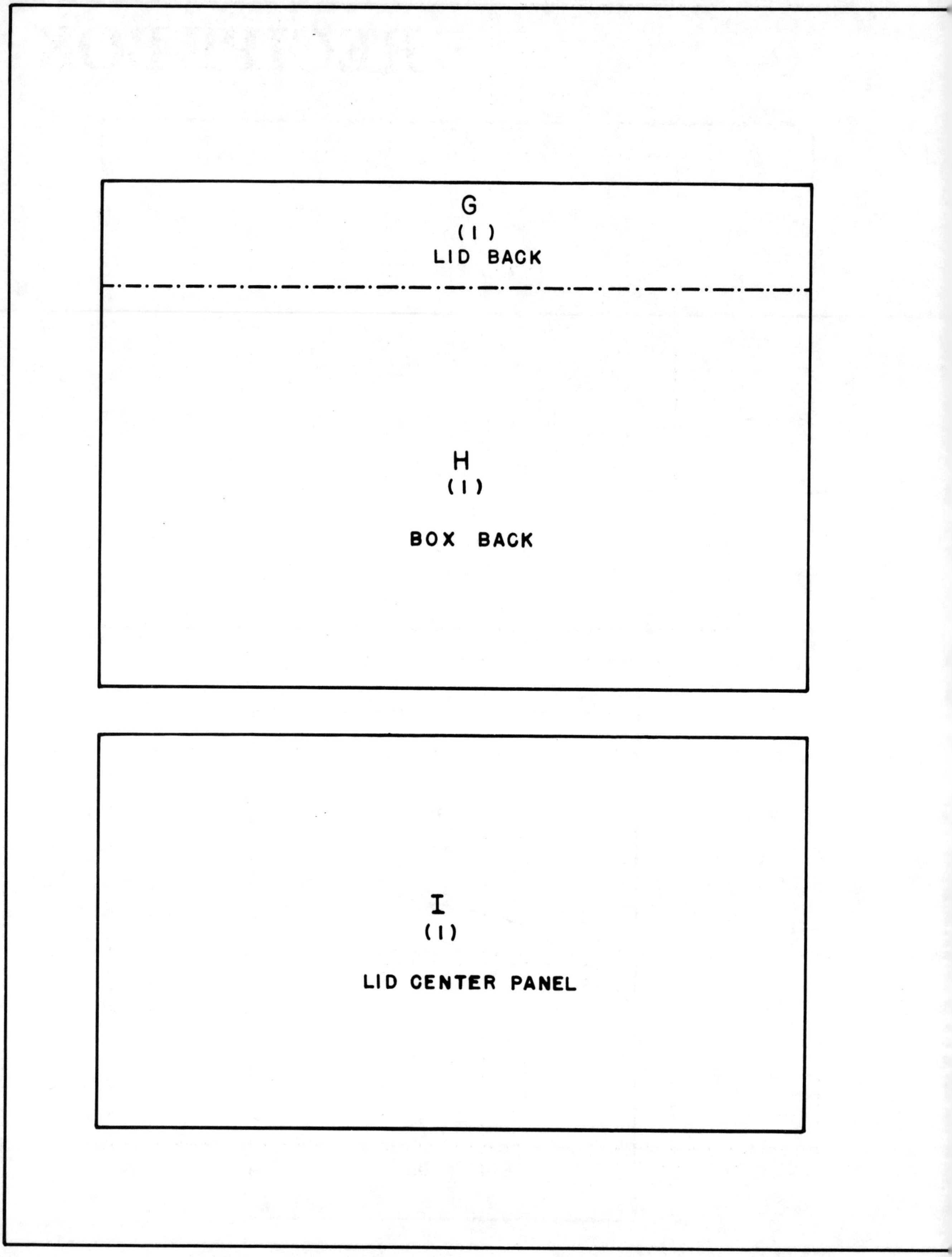

G
(1)
LID BACK

H
(1)

BOX BACK

I
(1)

LID CENTER PANEL

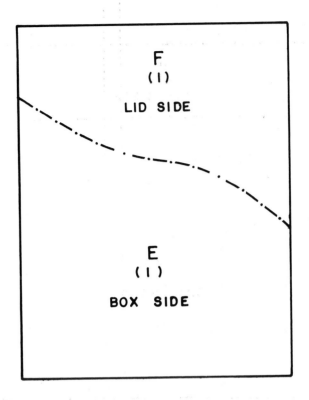

F
(1)

LID SIDE

E
(1)

BOX SIDE

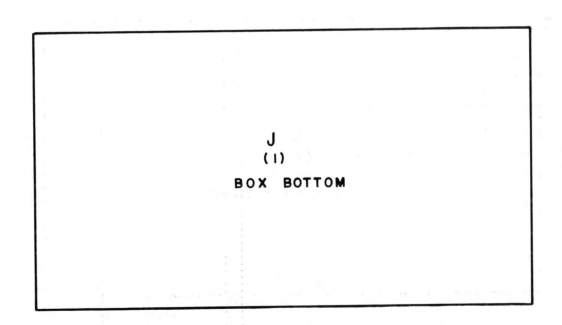

J
(1)

BOX BOTTOM

Pattern 9

FINISHED SIZE: 9¼" x 5" x 2¼" high.

APPROXIMATE TIME FOR COMPLETION: Four hours.

RECOMMENDED GLASS: Panel "B", ½ square foot double strength mirror. "A" panels may be made in the glass of your choice. The lid will require approximately ½ square foot of glass, depending upon the design that you select.

PROCEDURE:

1. Accurately cut and foil the "A" and "B" panels.

2. Lay out five of the "A" panels in a straight line, and rigidly attach them to each other. Tack these five "A" panels to the straight edge of the "B" panel. The ends of the five "A" panels will extend slightly beyond the ends of the straight edge of the "B" panel. Tack one additional "A" panel to the center of the curved front edge of the "B" panel (see reference point marked on the pattern. Begin tacking the rest of the "A" panels, one at a time, to either side of the front "A" panel, until all of the remaining "A" panels are attached around the edge of the "B" panel. There will be some gaps between the "A" panels and the edge of the "B" panel as you fit them into or around the curves of the "B" panel. You may also have a small gap at either side of the initial five "A" panels that you attached. This is due to differences in glass thicknesses used in the sides. Simply fill this gap with solder when final beading. It should be no more than ¼". When you are satisfied with the alignment of all panels, you may final bead all seams and edges.

3. Patina and wash the structure.

4. Place the finished box upside down over the bottom ("B") pattern. Make any adjustment necessary. Design a pattern within this template. Cut and foil all lid pieces. Remember that they can not grow beyond or alter the shape of the initial template. Solder these pieces together to form the lid. Remember also that this template represents the reverse side of the lid, so cut and solder accordingly.

5. Hinge, patina, add finishing accents and chain, and thoroughly wash according to the recommendations in the text.

Due to the irregular shape of the lid and box, it is easiest if the hinge tube is added to the back edge of the lid, rather than the back edge of the box. This allows the hinge rods to fall down into the back seams of the box, avoiding the need to bend the rod into an irregular shape.

A
(26)
SIDES

Fan Shell Box

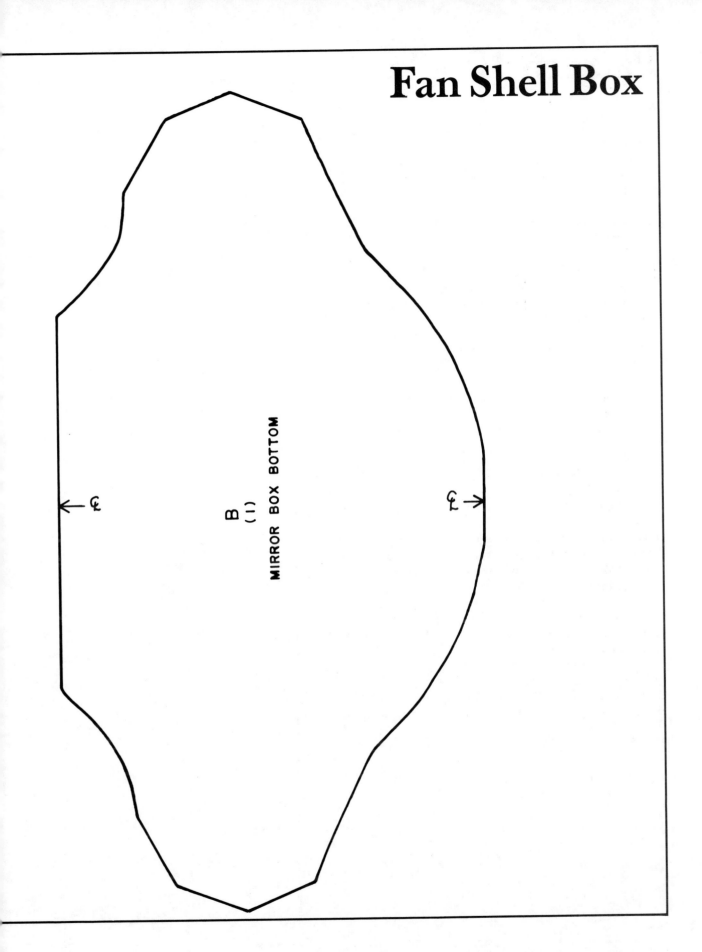

B
(1)
MIRROR BOX BOTTOM

¢L

¢L

Pattern 10

FINISHED SIZE: 10½" x 4" high.

APPROXIMATE TIME FOR COMPLETION: Five hours.

RECOMMENDED GLASS: ¼ square foot (6"x 6") double strength mirror for panel "D". Panels "A" and "C": 1¼ square feet glass of your choice. Panels "B": ¾ square foot accent glass of your choice. The lid "E" requires a total of approximately ¾ square foot glass (8"x 8"). The design is of your choice.

PROCEDURES:

1. Accurately cut and foil panels "A", "B", "C", and "D".
2. Lay the six "A" panels face down in a fan configuration on your work surface (Figure 1). Carefully align all panels and lightly tack at all meeting corners (Figure 2). Draw the ends of the fan up and together, forming a cone. Tack at remaining corners. Lightly bead the inside seams of the cone. Set this "A" cone aside. Repeat this process with the "C" panels. Form two "B" cones with the "B" panels. You should now have four cones.
3. Place the "D" panel inside the small diameter opening of the "A" ring. Tack into place. Lower one "B" ring, matching like dimensions. Align all panels and tack in place. Turn this structure over on the work surface and make sure that the edge of the "B" ring fits flush with the work surface. This will give you a straight edge to align with the top. If it does not fit flush, adjust any "B" panels necessary to achieve a straight edge. When everything is straight and aligned, you may set the structure aside and proceed with the next step.
4. Place the "C" ring, small diameter down, on your work surface. Attach the second "B" ring to its upper edge in the same manner as with the structure in Step 3. Again turn this structure over on the work surface to check that the edge of the "B" ring is flat. You will not have added the "E" panel at this time. Make any adjustments necessary.

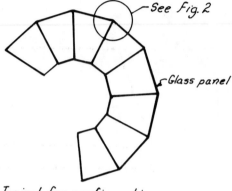

Typical fan configuration
Fig. 1

Typical corner tack, top & bottom
Fig. 2

Clam Shell Box

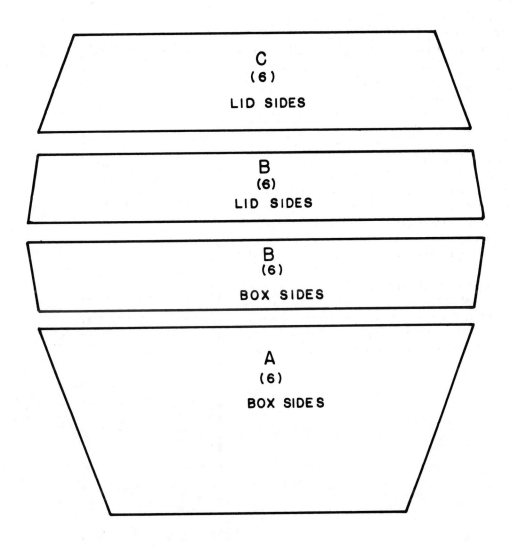

5. Now take the structure from Step 3 and place it on the work surface, large diameter up. Lower the structure from Step 4, large diameter down, onto the upper edge of it. Do all of the edges meet? If not, make any adjustments necessary. When you are satisfied with the alignment of all panels, separate the two sections.

6. You man now final bead all remaining seams and edges, inside and out, except for the space into which the "E" panel will fit.

7. The "E" panel may now be cut as patterned or a design may be made within its perimeters. It is advisable to set the opening in the structure over the "E" panel pattern to assure the fit. Make any adjustment necessary to the pattern. Cut and foil the panel of pieces. Be sure that the panel size does not grow if it contains a design.

8. Tack the panel together and in place. Remember that the panel pattern represents the underside of the lid panel, so be sure to take this into consideration when cutting the design.

9. With the panel in place, you may final bead all remaining seams.

10. Hinge, add any desired accents, patina and thoroughly wash the box according to the procedures detailed in the text. Due to the heavier weight of some lids, it may be best to omit the addition of a chain to this box. If hinging is done according to the text, then the lid should easily lay backward onto the work surface without binding.

Clam Shell Box

D
(I)

MIRROR BOX BOTTOM
TEMPLATE

E
(I)

LID CENTER PANEL
TEMPLATE

Appendix A—The Ruler

You are not alone if you have problems reading measurements on a ruler. Many stained glass workers have difficulty in reading increments smaller than an inch on a ruler. This section is designed to help you cope with the problem. Knowledge of the proper use of a ruler is essential in the design and creation of geometric structures. All of us use measurements during our day-to-day activities, but seldom do we get into measurements as small as 16ths or 32nds. You will, however, use these measurements in geometric design. Measurements this small are often critical in the fit of one piece to another, or a tray within a box. Reading a ruler is really quite easy once you get used to working with fractions.

The fractions are indicated by the height of the line on the ruler as shown in Figure A-1. The highest line is for the full inch increment. The second highest line is for one-half ($1/2$) inch increments. The third highest line is one-quarter ($1/4$) inch increments. Notice that there are three of these lines. The fourth $1/4$ inch line falls on the next full inch increment.

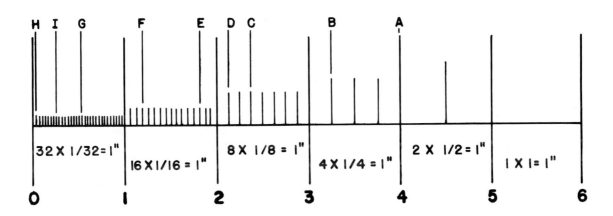

A-1   The Ruler

The next highest line is for one-eighth ($1/8$) inch, the next for one-sixteenth ($1/16$) inch, and the shortest line is for one-thirty-second ($1/32$) inch. Some rulers have smaller increments ($1/64$), not shown here, using an even shorter line.

Study the illustration above and try to read measurements "A" through "I".

A . . . . 4.0"
B . . . . 3-1/4"
C . . . . 2-3/8"
D . . . . 2-1/8"
E . . . . 1-13/16"
G . . . . 17/32"
H . . . . 1/32"
I . . . . 8/32"
($4/16$" or $2/8$" or $1/4$". These measurements are all the same. They represent using different, yet equal denominations.)

Please read Appendix B for further help in coping with fractions which will assist you in reading rulers.

Appendix B—Fraction Conversions

Working with fractions is something many of us have managed to avoid since we left school. Since the use of fractions is an important part in the design and construction of boxes, I have given you a conversion chart for many of the common fractions used in the text. I also will attempt to briefly explain the methods of converting other fractions. A fraction, in the sense that I use it, is a portion of an inch. Most rulers are broken into 32nds of an inch. Each inch contains thirty-two (32) 32nds. Therefore one inch could be referred to as $^{32}/_{32}$; one half inch would equal $^{16}/_{32}$, since there are only one-half the number of 32nds in a half inch. Likewise, there are sixteen (16) 16ths in one inch and eight (8) 16ths in a half inch.

At times, you may have to convert quarters into 32nds. This is done by dividing four (4) into 32. The answer is 8. This means that in each quarter of an inch, there are $^8/_{32}$nds. If you want to know how many 32nds are in $^3/_4$", simply multiply three (3) by eight (8). The answer is 24. Therefore, $^3/_4$" would equal $^{24}/_{32}$". This method can be used to arrive at the figures I have given in the Fraction Conversion Chart, Figure B-1. Other examples are:

$^3/_4$ ¾ $^6/_8$ or $^{12}/_{16}$
$^7/_8$ ¾ $^{14}/_{16}$ or $^{28}/_{32}$
$^3/_{16}$ ¾ $^6/_{32}$
$^3/_8$ ¾ $^6/_{16}$ or $^{12}/_{32}$

	Halves	Forths	Eighths	Sixteenths	Thirty Seconds
1"	$^2/_2$	$^4/_4$	$^8/_8$	$^{16}/_{16}$	$^{32}/_{32}$
$^1/_2$"	$^1/_2$	$^2/_4$	$^4/_8$	$^8/_{16}$	$^{16}/_{32}$
$^1/_4$"		$^1/_4$	$^2/_8$	$^4/_{16}$	$^8/_{32}$
$^1/_8$"			$^1/_8$	$^2/_{16}$	$^4/_{32}$
$^1/_{16}$"				$^1/_{16}$	$^2/_{32}$
$^1/_{32}$"					$^1/_{32}$

B-1   Fraction Conversions

Appendix C—The Protractor

The protractor is a tool used to determine the angular relationship of one line to another. It is usually in the form of a half circle on clear plastic. Since a full circle is broken into 360 degrees, the protractor is divided into 180 degrees, as shown in Figure C-1.

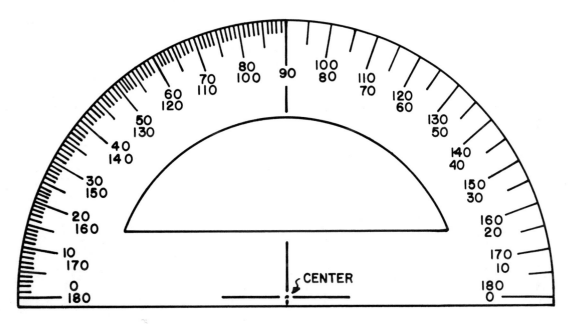

C-1   The Protractor

These degrees represent a position's relationship to horizontal. You will notice that the vertical line that intersects the horizontal line (0o-180o) is at 90 degrees. The larger the number, the greater the angle. You will notice that each main section has two numbers which, when added together, equal 180. This is because a line intersects another line at two angles, with respect to the degrees in a whole.

If you were told to cut something at 70 degrees, you would be leaving a remainder of 110 degrees. Angles that appear sharp or pointed are less than 90 degrees. Figure C-2 shows examples of various angles.

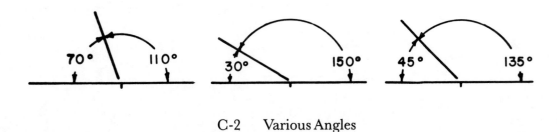

C-2   Various Angles

Glossary

BEAD LINE—a continuous run of solder along a seam or edge of the structure.

DEPTH—The measurement from the front to the back of a structure.

FINISHED BEAD—A raised layer of solder added over the copper foil in a rounded, smooth, or textured line.

HEIGHT—The measurement from top to bottom of a structure.

HEXAGON—A geometric figure with six sides and six angles.

HORIZONTAL—Parallel to the plane of the horizon; flat and even, level.

INSIDE PERIMETER—The inside lines of a place or structure.

OCTAGON—A geometric figure with eight angles and eight sides.

OUTSIDE PERIMETER—The outside lines of a place or structure.

PARALLEL—Two lines or planes running at equal distance from one another.

PENTAGON—A geometric figure with five sides and five angles.

PERPENDICULAR—At right angles (90 degrees) to another plane or line.

PLANE—A flat surface.

POLYGON—Any geometric figure with more than four sides and angles.

RECTANGLE—A four sided figure with all angles at 90 degrees, with two sides of one length and two sides of another length.

RIGHT ANGLE—90 degrees.

SQUARE—A four-sided geometric figure with four 90 degree angles and four sides of equal length; at 90 degrees to something.

TACK—To lightly attach one piece of glass to another with a thin spot or layer of solder.

TIN—To lightly coat the entire foil surface with a thin layer of solder.

TRAPEZOID—A geometric figure with four sides with only two parallel sides.

TRIANGLE—A geometric figure with three sides and three angles.

VERTICAL—Perpendicular or at a 90 degree angle to the horizon.

WIDTH—The measurement from one side of a structure to the other side.

Index

Other Books from Aurora:

ART GLASS IMAGES by Thomas Morin, II This book contains 67 truly superlative designs, each intended for large format construction. It contains a wide variety of designs: 21 Flower designs; 12 bird designs; 9 animal designs; 5 plant and tree designs; 7 sea and landscape designs; plus many more fresh, innovative designs. Eleven of the designs are shown in beautiful full-color photos. This book also contains a 9-page section with 15 illustrations on enlarging, reshaping, simplifying and adapting designs, by Trudy Thomas, author of "Decorative Soldering."

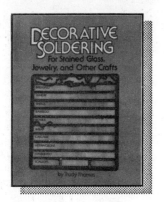

DECORATIVE SOLDERING FOR STAINED GLASS, JEWELRY, AND OTHER CRAFTS by Trudy Thomas

This book provides instructions on a revolutionary new technique which adds a truely new dimension to the stained glass craft. The technique not only enables the stained glass artisan to dress up their windows and boxes, but also to create beautiful jewelry and sculptures using found objects, stones, and stained glass in imaginative and exciting new forms.

**AURORA STAINED GLASS PATTERNS
BOOK 1 — Knights, Dragons, Etc. by Amy Flores**

This book feature 8 full-sized (up to 11" X 16-1/2") patterns on heavy-duty paper, perforated for easy removal from the book. Color photographs of each project, executed in stained glass, are shown on the cover. These projects make exciting gifts for children, or anyone who is interested in the adventures of King Arthur and his round table. The projects may be executed in either lead or copper foil.

**AURORA STAINED GLASS PATTERNS
BOOK 2 — Frames & Mirrors by Amy Flores**

This book feature 8 full-sized (up to 11" X 16-1/2") patterns on heavy-duty paper, perforated for easy removal from the book. Color photographs of each project, executed in stained glass, are shown on the cover. These designs may be used as either frames or mirrors. When used as frames, the picture area may be broken up into smaller areas with lead lines to show groups of smaller photographs. The projects may be executed in either lead or copper foil.